Gospel of the Kingdom

Exploring the Gospel of Mark

— PATRICK WHITWORTH —

Sacristy
Press

Sacristy Press
PO Box 612, Durham, DH1 9HT

www.sacristy.co.uk

First published in 2021 by Sacristy Press, Durham

Sacristy Limited, registered in England & Wales, number 7565667

British Library Cataloguing-in-Publication Data
A catalogue record for the book is available from the British Library

ISBN 978-1-78959-179-8

*Dedicated to the memory of
Nicholas Maude,
who memorized and dramatically presented
St Mark's Gospel.*

Contents

Foreword

I have been very fortunate to sit at Patrick's feet for three series of his talks. His style is always insightful, prayerful and authoritative, combined with a lightness and humour which makes them engaging and compelling. You can imagine my delight when he asked me to write this foreword for what is my passion, Mark's Gospel.

All too often it seems that, for preachers and writers alike, Matthew and Luke are the go-to Synoptic Gospels for quotes and text. Mark on the other hand is often overlooked. But read through Mark, and you will find a pacey and thrilling Gospel, each story packed with detail and meaning.

Compare, for instance, the healing of the demon-possessed man and the Gadarene swine, told in all three. Luke describes it thus:

> When Jesus stepped ashore, he was met by a demon-possessed man from the town. For a long time this man had not worn clothes or lived in a house, but had lived in the tombs.
>
> *Luke 8:27*

From Mark we have:

> When Jesus got out of the boat, a man with an impure spirit came from the tombs to meet him. This man lived in the tombs, and no one could bind him anymore, not even with a chain. For he had often been chained hand and foot, but he tore the chains apart and broke the irons on his feet. No one was strong enough to subdue him. Night and day among the tombs and in the hills he would cry out and cut himself with stones.
>
> *Mark 5:2–5*

So much more vivid, and so much more evocative of the power of the force confronting Jesus, with what surely must be eyewitness detail. It is this and the thrill, pace and urgency of the Gospel that Patrick captures so well in this urgent and pacey guide.

It was this power and excitement of Mark's Gospel that inspired me to learn it by heart, as a way of trying to get to know Jesus better for myself, and then try to bring that power and excitement to others by devising a dramatic presentation, which I have now done over thirty times.

In learning and performing the Gospel, two particular things have struck me, both of which are apparent in Patrick's new interpretation. The first is how the Word is living and even ten years after beginning to learn it I am seeing new ideas and connections. The second relates to those connections and how there is a cohesion to the whole Gospel, with certain different narratives becoming evident as the Gospel is told.

The joy of learning the Gospel by rote, chewing over each phrase, verse, story and chapter again and again, was literally "letting the word of Christ dwell in me richly". As I went through, new things kept striking me, and even now, after each performance something fresh will emerge, such is the power of the living word. Patrick's book has shown me much more besides, especially his emphasis on the context of first-century Rome, where it is very likely to have been written, and the contrast he makes between the worldly imperial kingdom and the heavenly kingdom Jesus came to establish. In my dramatized performance, the setting, as well, is imperial Rome, Peter having just been martyred. I play Mark—who might well be next—dictating furiously and urgently into the night to record this most precious story.

Hearing only small sections of the Gospel, as we do normally, means so much gets lost from the wider arc of the Gospel, of the connections between stories and the developing climax as the journey of Jesus, beginning in Galilee, leads in the second half relentlessly towards Jerusalem and the cross, from the first proclamation of the kingdom to the climax of its fulfilment.

Viewing it as a whole you see that so much of it is written from Peter's perspective and that he has the prominence of being the first and last-named apostle. Furthermore, the "warts and all" portrayal of Peter by Mark hints at its coming directly from Peter himself. All of this gives further evidence for Peter being the main source for Mark, while you also see the importance of eyewitness as a whole, there generally being named or anonymous, explicit or implicit eyewitnesses in every scene, as if Mark anticipates the scepticism of his audience.

Viewing it as whole you also begin to get a wonderful portrait of the true identity of Jesus, why he came and what it means to follow him. Rarely does Mark describe him directly, but holds a mirror, that mirror being the reactions of others, be it the religious authorities, the disciples, the crowds, his family, certain individuals or the evil spirits. It is arguable that for Mark the climax of the Gospel is not the resurrection, but the reaction of the pagan Roman centurion at the foot of the cross: "Surely this man was the Son of God" (15:39). Jesus' power, charisma, majesty, authority, his divinity—but also his deep humanity—emerge strongly as he strides though the Gospel.

By taking us through long sections of the Gospel at a time, Patrick likewise explores many such overarching narratives, making fascinating and helpful connections throughout, not just within Mark's Gospel but between the Gospels and with the Old Testament, while all the time making that connection with the early Church and first-century Rome.

Halfway through the Gospel, in Mark 8:29, Jesus challenges the disciples by asking: "Who do you say I am?" This is a question that is vital for us all, and answering it is our lifetime's pilgrimage.

Mark's answer is simple: "The beginning of the good news about Jesus the Messiah, the Son of God" (1:1). He is bringing us the life-transforming good news of Jesus Christ, the Son of God, and through the evidence of Peter and all the eyewitnesses, he wants our lives to be transformed as well.

Reading Mark's Gospel is a powerful and thrilling way for us to better get to know Jesus for ourselves. Patrick's account of it brings us an invaluable new interpretation, set in the historical context which he knows so well, and with his prayerful and inspiring insight and authority, it is an indispensable guide to that life-transforming good news.

The Revd Canon Gerald Osborne
Pewsey, June 2021

Preface

This is now the third in a series on the Gospels. Two previous books have been published in this series on the Gospels of Luke and of Matthew. With so many books already published on the Gospels, why another one? The purpose of this series is to look at each Gospel from the point of view of its unique message: that is not only in recording the life and ministry of Jesus but also the particular standpoint or perspective of each Gospel writer. Hence, I called Matthew the *Gospel of Fulfilment*, since Matthew, writing in the first instance for Jewish Christians, was at pains to show how Jesus fulfilled all Old Testament expectations and how the message of Jesus' kingdom was to make disciples throughout the world—and Matthew explains powerfully what that meant, for example in the Sermon on the Mount. Luke, I called the *Gospel for the Outsider*. Luke was most probably a Gentile himself. He had travelled extensively with the Apostle Paul evangelizing the cities of Asia and Europe and had gained access to material from women, notably from Mary the Mother of Jesus and Elizabeth the mother of John the Baptist, which he uniquely included. There seems to be a focus too both in the narrative and the parables (such as the Parables of the Good Samarian and the Prodigal Son) on the outsider or marginalized, whether Gentiles, Roman soldiers, criminals or the excluded.

With regard to Mark the distinguishing feature seems to be the embodiment and proclamation of a new kingdom which lies at the centre of Jesus' teaching. Written most probably in Rome, Mark had the testimony of Peter, which he faithfully recorded but now vividly understood in the context of the the buildings, events and politics of the imperial power of Rome. And a Rome which, after Tiberius, was facing the tempestuous politics of the reigns of Claudius, Caligula and Nero. In that context, how different was the kingdom announced by Jesus and proclaimed by Mark, a kingdom of service, self-sacrifice, humility and faithfulness! A truly revolutionary kingdom that would challenge and subvert all human wielding of power!

Mark's Gospel is peculiarly compelling, dramatic and immediate. It is breathless in its narrative and profound in its message. It therefore has lent itself to dramatic performance or retelling by people who memorized it in its entirety. I have been fortunate to listen, and be moved by, several such notable performances. In my twenties, I heard Alec McCowen perform Mark's Gospel at the Mermaid Theatre in the West End of London. In Bath, where I worked for twenty years, I heard Lloyd Notice perform in our rectory garden for over a hundred on a summer's evening. I have heard Gerald Osborne, an ordained farmer, who has kindly written the Foreword to this book, perform it in Bath Abbey. And I have dedicated this book to the memory of Nicholas Maude, who died much too young aged fifty-eight, but not before learning and dramatically presenting the whole of this Gospel on many occasions, including in front of Alec McCowen CBE, and in our own church at All Saints, Bath Weston. All of them have scattered the seed of the word in order to give growth to the kingdom (Mark 4:1–20).

I would like to thank them, Benedict Books for reviewing early drafts, Natalie Watson, my editor at Sacristy Press, and my family for further absences to bring it to fruition.

Patrick Whitworth
10 June 2021

Introduction

This is the third in a series of studies on the four Gospels, with the last, on the fourth Gospel, still to be written. The purpose of the series is to give the reader the *unique selling point* of each Gospel. This concept is derived from the idea that each of the four Gospel writers is telling the story of Jesus from a particular standpoint. Matthew, the most Jewish of all the Gospels, was written with the aim of demonstrating that, in Jesus, everything *promised* in the Old Testament is *fulfilled*: the law, the sacrificial system, the prophecies about the life of the Messiah and his ministry—particularly as the Son of Man (Daniel) and the Suffering Servant (Isaiah). The Early Church placed this Gospel first in the New Testament, with the idea that it forms a bridge between the Old Testament and the New. Thus, the way Matthew edited the Gospel, gathered the material about Jesus—most probably in Antioch—and placed it in his Gospel, reveals his purpose of telling everyone that Jesus was the Messiah who fulfilled all that went before. And this fact should now be the basis of a new community (the Church) and proclaimed to the world (Matthew 28:18–20).

If Matthew's is the *Gospel of Fulfilment*, then Luke's is the *Gospel of the Outsider*. Luke was most probably a Gentile. He travelled with Paul on his missionary journeys, even to Rome. He was a doctor, accustomed to observing and treating human frailties, both mental and physical. He readily identified with the stranger, the foreigner, the outsider and the failure. He gave us the Parables of the Prodigal Son and the Good Samaritan. In other words, he showed Jesus's compassion towards the sinner, and the grace that was available—nowhere more so than in Luke 15.

How then might the Gospel of Mark best be described? What was its unique selling point? For this series I have characterized it as the *Gospel of the Kingdom*. With a style that is immediate, compelling and explosive, Mark presents Jesus in a way that is both direct and transformational.

There are no considered beginnings and endings, simply raw news that forces readers to make up their own minds. It is quite possible that the urgency in Mark's writing mirrors the urgency of his own situation, in which the Christian community was facing increasing pressure, quite possibly where he was in Rome. Perhaps the Gospel was never quite finished as the net of persecution closed in and various people wrote different endings as a result (something we will come to). As with other Gospel writers, the style of the book, its intention and structure, are the result of the background, experiences and convictions of the author and his own interaction with Jesus, either direct or indirect.

One further characteristic of Mark's Gospel from the outset was the hostility of the Teachers of the Law (see 2:6ff.) which was matched only by the obtuseness of the disciples, who continually misunderstood Jesus's and their own calling. Neither understood the kingdom that Jesus was bringing, nor the nature of his new kind of kingship.

All theological writing—and a Gospel is theological writing—springs from the worldview of the author. Mark's worldview (how he thought about the world, creation, God, humanity, salvation and the future) was derived from his experiences and reflections. We also know from what Scripture says about itself, that the Spirit moves people to give us the inspired word of God through the process of human reflection. In other words, the words written on the page are both human and God-breathed, and through these words God may continually address the human family. This gives Scripture its revelatory power and authority. And so it is time to look at the life and personality of the author of the Gospel of Mark, a Gospel characterized by the Early Church with the symbol of the lion.

Who was Mark?

Mark himself weaves in and out of the story of the Early Church, with snippets found in the Acts of the Apostles and in Paul's Epistles. It is fair to say that he was a slightly controversial character. Mark, or John Mark, may even have made an anonymous appearance in his own Gospel. A number of scholars believe that the figure who slips out of his robe at the arrest of Jesus, leaving the garden of Gethsemane naked, is indeed

Mark (Mark 14:51, 52). It is speculation, but if true, we know that he was already a follower of Jesus and an eyewitness of the passion that figures so largely in his Gospel.

However, Mark officially enters the story of the Early Church as a colleague of Barnabas. Barnabas (a nickname meaning Son of Encouragement) was a merchant from Cyprus, a member of the tribe of Levi, and was called Joseph. Like Mark's family (see Acts 12:12ff.), Barnabas had property in Jerusalem that he sold before giving the proceeds to the Church, laying it at the apostles' feet (Acts 4:36, 37). Mark, or John Mark as he is sometimes called, may have been connected to the Jewish merchant class with links to the diaspora in Cyprus, and in particular to Cyrene, present-day Libya. Mark makes it clear that he knows the family of Simon of Cyrene, and especially his sons, Alexander and Rufus (Mark 15:21). Rufus may also have been in Rome (Romans 16:13). As a follower of Jesus and a relative of Barnabas he was a natural companion for Barnabas and Paul on their first missionary journey to Cyprus and the province of Galatia (Acts 13ff.). Yet this is where a controversy began.

For some unexplained reason, John Mark deserted Paul and Barnabas while they were in Pamphylia, which is the region nearest the coast, so presumably this was early on in the mission. A quarrel ensued between Paul and Barnabas: Barnabas wanted to take his cousin on the next missionary journey, but Paul would not take someone who had previously turned back. We are told it was a sharp disagreement (Acts 15:39), with Barnabas living up to his name and determined to give his cousin a second chance. Paul, the ever-focussed strategist, was not prepared to take that risk. They parted company but were later reconciled. We find that Mark subsequently re-joined Paul and was with him when he was writing his letter to the Colossians during Paul's first imprisonment in Rome (Colossians 4:10). Later, when nearing the end of his life, Paul wrote in his second letter to Timothy: "Get Mark and bring him with you, because he is helpful in my ministry" (2 Timothy 4:11). Whatever the past problem between them, Paul was now reconciled to Mark, although his words do sound a little imperious. What is clear however is that Mark did return to Rome, and there he became an associate of the Apostle Peter. And it was with Peter's help and in Rome that the idea of the Gospel was most probably conceived.

There is one final part of Mark's story which must be considered, which is his founding of the Church in Egypt. Speak to any Coptic Christian and they are quite sure that Mark was responsible for its founding. The Coptic tradition is that Mark came to Alexandria, where he preached and founded a church between AD 39 and 50.[1] There are other references to Mark being in Egypt from Clement of Alexandria and John Chrysostom, who maintains that Mark wrote his Gospel in Egypt. In summary, what we can say is that there is an Early Church tradition from the fourth century of Mark preaching in Egypt and most probably in Alexandria, but details about when, to what effect and for how long are very sketchy. However, it is more likely to have been before his time in Rome and before his Gospel was fully written, with the benefit of Peter's reminiscences being firmly at its core.

Peter, Mark and Rome

The clue to Mark's arrival in Rome comes in the Apostle Peter's first letter (1 Peter 5:13), where Mark, who is described as Peter's "son", sends greetings to the recipients of the letter in Pontus, Galatia, Cappadocia, Asia and Bithynia (1 Peter 1:1). Peter describes Rome as Babylon. We don't know how long Mark stayed with Peter in Rome—possibly a year or two. At the same time, as we have seen, Paul requested Mark to come to him as he was imprisoned in Rome (see 2 Timothy 4:11). What we know for sure is that Mark lived with Peter in Rome, if not in the same house, at least within the Christian community there. The community had reassembled after its eviction in the time of the Emperor Claudius.[2] We also know that during this time, probably during the reign of Nero (AD 54–68), the Church was under increasing pressure and soon to experience a great wave of persecution, with Christians made scapegoats for all the ills of Nero's rule, especially the great fire of Rome in AD 64.

Two things follow from Mark's stay in Rome and his closeness to the Apostle Peter. Firstly, Mark repeatedly heard the stories Peter told of the life, ministry and passion of Jesus, and more than that, it appears that Mark was Peter's secretary or "interpreter", writing down these stories and teachings for use after Peter's death. Indeed, one Bishop of Hierapolis,

Papias, wrote after the "publication" of the Gospel of Mark that Mark was Peter's "interpreter". Thus, it had become known in the Early Church that Mark was writing down Peter's record of life with Jesus over those three years of his ministry. The second thing is that, while staying in Rome, Mark had ample time to draw a living contrast between the kingdom of his Lord and Christ and the kingdoms of this world, principally that of imperial Rome.

Both points are foundational in understanding Mark's Gospel. There is a vividness to the Gospel, and an urgent and compelling tone, hence the repeated use of the adverb *immediately*, which comes directly from the eyewitness details of the text. The impact of the eyewitness is nowhere stronger than in the account of Jesus calming the storm (Mark 4:35–41), or walking on the water (Mark 6:45ff.), although curiously Mark does not tell us of Peter's momentary attempt to walk on the water himself (see Matthew 14:22–36). Perhaps Peter did not care to dwell on his panicky ducking. Instead, Peter gives Mark his stories of Jesus's ministry and passion, which the scholars call *pericopai*.

As with other ancient biographies, Mark's biography of Jesus threads these snapshot stories together, like pearls on a gold chain. The gold chain is of course principally the personality and power of Jesus, but it is also his main message about the coming of the kingdom. The reality of that kingdom juxtaposed against all earthly rule, and in particular imperial Rome, is given heightened contrast, definition and meaning from Mark being in Rome at the time the Gospel was assembled. Many scholars think that the Gospel was written before the destruction of Jerusalem in AD 70, quite possibly soon after Peter's execution, and as a record of all that Mark had learnt from the Apostle.

The experience of Rome

For a moment let us imagine the effect living in Rome might have had on Mark. It is interesting to note *en passant* how many of the New Testament writers spent time in Rome. There was, it appears, a kind of gravitational pull on these authors. Paul, Peter, Mark and Luke all spent time in Rome. A story that was based in Israel was told against the background of Rome. Indeed, it was a Roman governor, a Roman method of execution (crucifixion) and Roman soldiers who were responsible for the central moment in Christ's life, his death, thus underlining the interaction between Rome and Israel, between the Empire of Rome and the kingdom of the Messiah (Christ).

If Mark lived in Rome for a year or more, there would have been many things he would have observed about the imperial city. Nero was the Emperor (AD 54–68), and before the Great Fire of AD 64, for which Christians were blamed and persecuted, the city was much as it had been during the years of Emperor Augustus (27 BC–AD 14). Surely Mark must have wandered through those clogged streets, host to over a million people, to the Palatine Hill. He would have seen the Temples of Jupiter and Concord close together, and the Gemonian Stairs where the bodies of enemies of the state were often found garrotted. He would have passed the Senate House where the likes of Cicero, Brutus, Julius Caesar and Cato could be easily recalled. Before the fire, he may even have passed close by the emperors' houses, whether belonging to Augustus, Tiberias or Nero. Near the Mausoleum of Augustus was the Altar of Peace, or the *Ara Pacis*, in which Rome herself is presented as the arbiter and bringer of peace. And if Mark had had a money belt on him and had fished out a coin to pay for food or some household goods in the *agora*, the coin would have borne the emperor's image and underneath the words *Divi filius* (Son of the Deified One or God). If, as a writer, he knew the works of Virgil (70–19 BC), the court poet, then he would have heard the great narrative that had been constructed, in which the genius of the emperor was depicted as the saviour of his people. According to Virgil, the emperor and his dynasty, the Julio-Claudians, channelled the spirit of Aeneas, a wandering, warrior Trojan who apparently founded Rome. Through these emperors, this spirit would now protect Rome and give the city unceasing victory.

If you were Mark, visiting Rome, staying with Peter who regarded you as his "son", how would you have written the Gospel, the "good news"? Who really was the *"Divi filius"*? Whose empire was really coming? Whose rule was permanent? Who truly brought peace? To whom did power belong? Whose house or *domus* would be eternal? Who would taste the banquet and enjoy the triumph to come? And how was an ordinary citizen, or even a slave—deemed of no worth except that which his or her master paid—to access and enjoy all these things? If Rome asked all the right questions, she gave all the wrong answers. So, Mark set himself to answer in his Gospel the questions everything around him in the imperial city and in his home city of Jerusalem begged. He would tell the story freely, briefly, bluntly and directly, threading what Peter had given him into a Gospel of unavoidable and explosive force.

CHAPTER 1

Start as You Mean to Go On

Mark 1

This book by Mark is all about good news. Mark makes this perfectly clear and repeats the same statement in verse 14 of the first chapter. The word he uses in his direct "*Daily Mail*" Greek is *euangelion*. We translate this with the word "gospel". *Euangelion* is good news or gospel. The next sixteen chapters will be a presentation of this good news. It is the Gospel that the apostles were bound to proclaim, and in doing so would tell the same story. Mark started his Gospel as he meant to go on, just as Jesus started his ministry as he meant to go on. It was that kind of ministry and, in keeping, that kind of Gospel.

Mark either did not have the sources or chose not to tell us about the birth of Jesus. Unlike Matthew and Luke, who gave us the story of Jesus's birth from Mary's point of view in Luke, and Joseph's point of view in Matthew, Mark's Gospel starts almost thirty years later when Jesus was already a grown man. He was embarking on his ministry, and from the outset there are two fundamental, principal things said about Jesus that grab our attention. He is the Messiah (the Christ), and he is the Son of God.

Each of the Gospel writers make these claims from the outset in different ways, but none quite so baldly as Mark. John uses almost philosophical language in saying Jesus was the Word made flesh (John 1:14). Matthew tells us he is Immanuel, God with us (Matthew 1:23). Luke tells us "He . . . will be called the Son of the Most High" (Luke 1:32). Mark plainly says that Jesus is firstly the Messiah and secondly the Son of God. The former is a statement for the Jewish world. The latter is a statement for the Gentile, pagan and Roman world. The life and passion of Jesus would overturn all conventional Jewish expectations of the Messiah. The life and passion of Jesus would also overturn all commonly held ideas of the Roman Gentile world about the *divi filius*, the Son of God. That Jesus would be entirely different from conventional expectations of the Messiah in the Jewish world would be good news once grasped, just as his being entirely different from all commonly held expectations of a Son of God in the Gentile world would also be good news. We will see why, as we go on. Reconfiguring those expectations in the Jewish and Gentile worlds would be painful, however.

Jesus is the Messiah, we are told, the *Christos*, which is simply the Greek for the chrismed one, the anointed one. To be anointed for a task by God was common currency, but nonetheless awesome. In the Old Testament, kings such as Saul and David were anointed (1 Samuel 10:1; 16:13). Aaron the Priest was anointed (Leviticus 8:12), and the prophet Elisha was anointed by Elijah in his place (1 Kings 19:16). Prophet, priest and king were all anointed for the task, and Jesus, as the Messiah, was anointed by his Father as Messiah. And we shall consider this at his baptism shortly. The giving of the Messiah to Israel was the pre-eminent sign of the faithfulness of God to his people Israel: all his promises to Israel were about to be finally and fully fulfilled in Jesus. Jesus was not the type of Messiah Israel was expecting because of his crucifixion—which ironically its leaders engineered and then objected to, and which became a scandal and stumbling block to them. But it was, in the wisdom of God, to be Israel's salvation (see 1 Corinthians 1:18–2:16). Mark tells us Jesus was the one Israel had been longing for, the Messiah. Israel was tinder dry in its expectation of a Messiah and now the spark had come.

To the Gentile world especially, Jesus was the Son of God, the *divi filius*. Perhaps Mark fingered a coin in his pocket, pushing his thumb over the raised imprint of the emperor's image, and then traced out the lettering of the claim that he, the emperor, was *divi filius* and said to himself, "it is simply not true". Nero, with his longing for praise, his play acting, his cruel ways, his unsatisfied desire for luxury, his killing of his mother, a Son of God?! No! thought Mark. I will tell you about the real Son of God, the *kosmokrator*—the real and true world ruler. Humans may wish to redraft the truth, but the reality is different.

Christendom's greatest church building, *Hagia Sophia*, is to be found in Istanbul. It was built on the site of a previous *Hagia Sophia*, where, as Bishop of Constantinople, the great Chrysostom (c. AD 347–407), or "golden mouth", was pastor and preacher until forced into exile by the unholy alliance of the Empress and the Bishop of Alexandria. Justinian rebuilt *Hagia Sophia* after a devastating fire in AD 557. Then, in 2020, the nationalist Turkish leader Recep Tayyip Erdoğan sought to convert it from a museum (designated as such by Atatürk) into a mosque. As Pope Francis and the Orthodox Patriarch said, the decision created deep disappointment and hurt among Christians. Muslims do not believe that Jesus is the Son of God. They do not believe that Christ suffered crucifixion. Yet the church had been built to worship Christ the Son of God and Christ the dying and rising Saviour. Nevertheless, whatever the intentions of governments or religious communities, the great mosaic of *Christos Pantocrator* looks down inside the church. However much people seek to redraft the truth, reality cannot be erased. Christ is *divi filius*, the *Pantocrator*, ruler over all, and remains as such in the mosaic of *Hagia Sophia*.

The announcer and the announcement (Mark 1:2–15)

The reality, as Mark says in the opening lines of his Gospel, is that Jesus is the Messiah and the Son of God. This would be announced and proclaimed in three ways: by John the Baptizer, by the voice of the Father at Jesus's baptism, and by the anointing of the Spirit.

Deep in Israel's history, in the eighth century BC, Isaiah had prophesied that there would be a voice of one crying in the wilderness: "Prepare the way for the Lord; make straight in the desert a highway for our God" (Isaiah 40:3).

Isaiah 40 is one of the great chapters of the Old Testament and marks a significant break in that prophetic book. Some scholars call Chapter 40 the beginning of Deutero-Isaiah (or Second Isaiah), where the prophet now addresses the people of Israel and tells them that their exile is coming to an end. He begins with those words that were set to music by Handel in his *Messiah*, "Comfort, comfort my people . . . Speak tenderly to Jerusalem, and proclaim to her that her hard service (exile) has been completed, that her sin has been paid for, that she has received from the Lord's hand double for all her sins" (Isaiah 40:1–2).

John the Baptist was Jesus's cousin and only a few months older than he. Their mothers had met when they were both pregnant (Luke 1:39ff.). And now John the Baptist fulfils the role spoken of him by Zechariah: "And you, my child, will be called a prophet of the Most High; for you will go on before the Lord to prepare the way for him, to give his people the knowledge of salvation through the forgiveness of their sins" (Luke 1:76). Wearing clothing made from camel hair and eating locusts and wild honey, John *announces* the Messiah, whose sandal straps he is unworthy to untie. He announces the end of Israel's exile, not from Babylon, which happened years ago, but exile from the close presence of God. Jesus will soon baptize with the Holy Spirit, whereas John may only baptize with water, signifying repentance and forgiveness, and this baptism of the Spirit will bring about a new intimate relationship that ends exile (see Ezekiel 36:24–32).

John announces a new beginning in the salvation history of God's people, the end of a spiritual exile. Yet a greater announcement is to come. As Jesus ascends out of the waters of baptism in the River Jordan, the Father speaks *personally* to Jesus, with the world eavesdropping: "You are my Son, whom I love; with you I am well pleased" (Mark 1:11). It is hard to put into words the significance of this affirmation (and we will return to the overall significance of the baptism of Jesus in a moment). They are words of deep assurance given at the outset of Jesus's ministry. Not only that, but as his head breaks the surface of the water, and he emerges to stand tall there, the Spirit anoints him, as a dove coming upon him (1:10).

Recently, I watched the sumptuously filmed BBC production of the Indian novel *A Suitable Boy*. One scene struck me especially: one of the principal characters stabs his best friend in a fit of jealous rage, thinking him a rival for the affections of the woman with whom he is infatuated. He gives himself up to the police and is imprisoned. His father's prospects as a politician are ruined from this dent to the family honour. In a gaol visit, the son asks the father if he still cares for him after the shame he has brought on the family. His father embraces him, and the son can now live with his shame, knowing he has not been abandoned. How much more

START AS YOU MEAN TO GO ON   13

the love of the Father of Lights for his totally innocent and obedient Son, "the Son whom I love"?

Jesus himself announced the coming of his kingdom. We are told he "went into Galilee, proclaiming the good news of God. 'The time has come, he said. The kingdom of God has come near. Repent and believe the good news'" (Mark 1:14, 15).

Every so often, when the royal family has some good news, be it a royal birth or a marriage, a notice is attached to the railings of Buckingham Palace. One day it may be sad news: the death of a member of the family, like for example the death of Prince Philip. When Jesus arrived in Galilee, he had good news to announce, however: "The kingdom of God has come near." It has come close with the presence of the king. The kingdom of God means the rule of God. If people are wanting a new type of government, a change of regime, his is a rule of justice, mercy, compassion, healing and truth. In him, such a kingdom has come close. There is only one response: repent and believe, that is, reorientate your life with him at the centre, and thereafter live a life of faith or trust. It is *always, ever, only* this response of faith that God looks for (see Habakkuk 2:4b). These are the true co-ordinates of Christian living.

As Jesus embarked on his ministry, leading inexorably to the passion and the cross as Mark makes plain, Jesus needed to be prepared, tested and equipped for what lay ahead. Mark tells us about this in typically terse form through his record of Jesus's baptism and temptations.

The baptism and temptations of Jesus

One of the great Renaissance paintings of the baptism of Jesus by John the Baptist is by the Quattrocento artist, Piero della Francesca, and it hangs in the National Gallery. In many ways Piero was a quiet revolutionary in his painting: reflective, perceptive and deeply spiritual, and is one of my favourite artists of that period. His depictions of the baptism of Jesus and of the resurrection of Jesus are both very memorable.

The picture we would say is "mannered", in that it is set in beautiful, serene Tuscan countryside near Piero's hometown of Sansepolcro, which can be seen in the distance. Jesus is being sprinkled with water from a delicate dish, rather than immersed, as he probably was, in the muddy waters of the Jordan. Yet the symmetry, mathematics and perspective are such that there is a vertical line through the picture that leads to heaven; a horizontal line that draws in the astonished onlookers, including the delightful angels; and a circle enclosing Jesus's loincloth, the tree beside him and the sky above. In other words, Piero's picture depicts the baptism involving the whole Godhead, with the Spirit above Jesus as a dove and the Father's presence in heaven implied. The moment is for the whole of humanity, with some getting ready for baptism and foreigners looking on, and with the created order represented by the walnut tree and the sky. In a word, the event is all encompassing.

The baptism of Christ was undoubtedly a moment when Jesus fully identified with his mission of redeeming humankind. In other Gospels, John the Baptist is reluctant to baptize Jesus, who is without sin and therefore in no need of repentance or cleansing. Yet Jesus sees it as part of his identification with the human beings he has come to save. Indeed, he says doing so fulfils righteousness, by which he means his Father's path for him (Matthew 3:15). And in Piero's painting, Jesus's expression is one of studied concentration and calm deliberation. For him this is the *beginning of an irreversible journey* in which the whole Godhead supports him: the Spirit anoints him beyond measure, and the Father affirms him as the beloved son in whom he is pleased. Jesus is ready. He is equipped.

As Gregory of Nyssa writes, "It is impossible to envisage any kind of severance or disjunction between them: one cannot think of the Son apart from the Father, nor divide the Spirit from the Son."[3] The Godhead is revealed at the baptism with the purpose of equipping Jesus for his ministry of making real and close the kingdom of God.

Yet if we think that burnished with such authority Jesus would have wafted his way into his ministry, we are mistaken. He was literally kicked out into the desert (the Greek word is *ekballen*), where he underwent fierce testing from the temptations of the Devil. Once again Mark does not enumerate or describe these. Perhaps he did not have a record of them from Peter. What we do know is that Jesus was in the wilderness for forty long days, a voluntary lockdown. He fasted, he was tested, he was offered shortcuts to popularity, power and momentary satisfaction. Instead, he kept to the way prescribed by his Father. As the writer to the Hebrews puts it, "He offered up prayers and petitions with fervent cries and tears to the one who could save him from death, and he was heard because of his reverent submission. Son though he was, he learned obedience from what he suffered" (Hebrews 5:7, 8).

We too have to learn the truth of what the Church Father Ignatius, Bishop of Antioch and martyr in Rome in AD 108, said: "Sin is our unwillingness to trust that God wants for us our deepest desires." Or to put it another way, he knows better than we know ourselves what is good for us.

Baptized and tested, Jesus was ready to start his ministry. He began as he meant to go on.

Jesus began as he meant to go on

In this remarkable opening chapter, there are several other ways in which Mark reveals the fundamentals of Jesus's ministry, and three in particular: the calling of a new community of disciples, the sacrament of healing, and the rhythm of prayer and activity in Jesus's own life. Let's take each in turn.

The call of the disciples

It is quite clear from the outset that Jesus is not going to minister alone; he is going to create a new community of disciples. To this end he soon sets about calling disciples to follow him. Four disciples are called from the lakeside of Galilee: Simon Peter and Andrew and James and John, two pairs of brothers. It is quite probable that the call of these disciples, as told by Mark, is a compressed story. Other Gospel writers fill out other parts of the narrative. In Chapter 5, Luke tells us of the great catch of fish that precedes the call of Simon Peter, James and John. John tells us that Simon Peter first meets Jesus by the River Jordan (see John 1:35ff.). Piecing these events and accounts together, we can see that Jesus's call of disciples, which is in fact the culmination of various interactions with Jesus, is baldly described by Mark.

Nevertheless, this is the decisive moment. They have seen and heard enough to decide. Jesus calls these four to leave and to follow him. They set aside their business and their work as fishermen. They leave their families and homes. They go out on an uncertain journey, pinning their hopes on Jesus, with maybe just half-formed ideas that he might be the Messiah. But there is something compelling and commanding about Jesus, such that staying would not just be a missed opportunity, but a denial of the very purpose of their existence. Peter will lead the Early Church and give Mark the content of his Gospel. John will become the beloved disciple, and write the fourth Gospel, before living to a great age in Ephesus, caring for Mary the mother of Jesus. James will die a martyr (Acts 12:2), and Andrew will be a missionary and possibly a martyr in Greece. There is no doubt that when they step away from their nets, they are embarking on an adventure of epic and unknown proportions, with their lives invested with a consequence far beyond fishing.

Later, twelve disciples will be formally appointed (Mark 3:13–19), with the express purpose of being "with [Jesus] and that he might send them out to preach and to have authority to drive out demons". They will indeed be sent out (6: 6b–13) and will learn the harsh truths that "a prophet" is not without honour, except in his own country, and that the fate of John the Baptist is a warning of the cost of discipleship (Mark 6).

Evidence of the kingdom

The second fundamental feature of Jesus's ministry is the healing that he brings to others through a new authority. Healing, although wonderful in itself, is also a sign or sacrament of something greater. It points to the kingdom of God, the bringing of the future into the present, the arrival of the rule of Jesus in the here and now, and a taste of what this kingdom or rule will be like.

The first instance of this in Mark's Gospel is the deliverance or healing of the man "with the impure spirit" in the synagogue in Capernaum (1:21–28). Mark highlights the authority of Jesus, to which we shall return in the next chapter. It is interesting to compare and contrast the different "first miracles" recorded in each of the Gospels. Matthew begins with a general description of Jesus's healing ministry (Matthew 4:23ff.) before proceeding to the same story about the healing of the leper as Mark (Mark 1:40–43), but only *after* the Sermon on the Mount (Matthew 8:1–4). Luke follows Mark with the story of the healing in the synagogue as the first miracle. John, however, records the miracle of turning water into wine (John 2:1-11). Each account reflects the priorities of the different Gospel writers. For Mark, the teaching Jesus gave that Sabbath in the synagogue was *not only in word but also in deed*. What Jesus says comes about. In other words, he is the God who said, "Let there be light," and there was light. And so too with a word he expels an evil spirit, and what he does for one he does for all who come to him (Mark 1:29-34). By the end of the chapter, Jesus has established that he is "willing" to heal, and motivated by compassion, he restores life, although his timetable is never dictated by human need alone.

A rhythm to life and work

The third feature of Jesus's ministry revealed in this opening sequence of Mark's Gospel is the rhythm of Jesus's life and work. He is not driven by human need alone. "Very early in the morning, while it was still dark, Jesus got up, left the house and went off to a solitary place, where he prayed" (Mark 1:35). What could be more instructive than his example?

Again and again during the pandemic of 2020, I heard people say that with possibilities of gathering for worship much diminished, they were forced to find places of solitude for their own prayers, meditation and reorientation. An active businessman wrote: "I have found this time of lockdown as time for solitude, re-examination and self-assessment." A busy mother and teacher spoke of the discipline of creating time for contemplation and withdrawal in her life. She quoted Isaiah 30:15: "In repentance and rest is your salvation, in quietness and trust is your strength, but you would have none of it." Well, far from fleeing *from* such a discipline, this mother has fled *into* it. In so doing she is following the example of Jesus, who through his times of prayer renewed his inner strength, refreshed his relationship with the Father, and prioritized his ministry for the coming day or days. Indeed, surely his response to the pressure of the statement, "Everyone is looking for you" (Mark 1:37)— with its subtext of, "what on earth have you been doing?"—was "let us go somewhere else". Released from the dictatorship of need he was able to embrace the freedom of obedience. And this freedom came through the channel of prayer.

Again and again in my study of the Early Church Fathers, I have been struck by their quest for silence, solitude and prayerfulness. Whether it be Basil of Caesarea, Gregory of Nazianzus or Gregory of Nyssa (collectively known as the Cappadocian Fathers), such was their delight. Likewise, Gregory the Great, the pope who sent Augustine to England in 597, considered that we should have about us the contemplation of a Mary and the activity of a Martha (Luke 10:38–42). Gregory writes in his *Pastoral Rule*: "The spiritual director should not reduce his attention to the internal life because of external occupations, nor should he relinquish his care for externals because of his anxiety for the internal life."[4] Jesus shows us the balance between the sustaining power of solitary prayer and the transforming exercise of spiritual authority: the two were and are intimately connected.

What an opening salvo is the first chapter of Mark's Gospel! It is as explosive as the events it describes. Jesus is introduced as the Messiah and Son of God. His arrival and ministry are prepared for by John the Baptist. He announces the proximity of the kingdom of God, for which repentance and faith are the only proper response. He begins his ministry as he means to go on: gathering to him disciples—the foundations of a new community; showing his authority by bringing healing to a man in the synagogue; and demonstrating the wellspring of his life, his prayer-dependent relationship with his Father. It is a breathless beginning to a dynamic telling of the good news.

CHAPTER 2

A New Authority

Mark 2 and 3

At two points in the account of the healing of the man with an impure spirit (Mark 1:22, 27) the crowd remarks that, unlike the teachers of the law, Jesus teaches and acts "with authority". Elsewhere we are told that the scribes and Pharisees "tie up heavy, cumbersome loads and put them on other people's shoulders, but they themselves are not willing to lift a finger to move them" (Matthew 23:4). By contrast, Jesus releases people such as this man with the impure spirit from their burdens.

Authority is an important concept in human society. Without its appropriate exercise, life would degenerate into chaos and confusion, in which the strongest or cleverest would suppress the more vulnerable. Indeed, without properly constituted authority, society can end up as the nightmare world of George Orwell's *Animal Farm*, where the bullies take control. In civil society, authority is granted by the state in accordance with the law. A prime minister has authority by virtue of a democratic election or by being chosen as leader by her or his party. Legislation has authority from its passage in the legislature. Lay officers, whether police or judges, are empowered to fulfil their tasks by virtue of being chosen for their office by the state, which also legally defines the extent of their powers.

But there are other forms of authority. Sometimes we say that so-and-so is an authority on art, ancient history or ceramics, by virtue of their knowledge. Other people appear to have moral authority through their consistent lifestyle. Still others have a kind of charismatic authority born of experience, and which is both personal and moral: Nelson Mandela was such a one. Authority therefore comes from a number of sources. For Jesus, authority came from his unique relationship with the Father.

Again, as Gregory of Nyssa wrote, "All that the Father is we see revealed in the Son; all that is the Son's is the Father's also. For the whole Son dwells in the Father, and he has the whole Father dwelling in himself."[5] This intermingling of the authority of the Father and the Son, and indeed the Spirit, is the basis of Jesus's authority.

Mark is able to demonstrate that this authority of Jesus is exercised in six ways: over his supernatural opponent, over the Sabbath, and over the created order, as well as in forgiving sins, calling others, and over sickness, the Devil and death. In all these areas, Jesus's authority was and is supreme. The purpose of using his authority was to reveal the nature of the kingdom of God, God's rule.

In this chapter, we will consider three aspects of Jesus's authority: his authority to forgive sins, his authority over the Sabbath, and his authority to call others. We will look at other areas of his authority in later chapters.

Authority to forgive sins

Forgiveness of sins is at the very heart of Jesus's mission. Indeed, it is in the meaning of his very name. His human father Joseph was told, "You are to give him the name Jesus (Yeshua or Joshua), because he will save his people from their sins" (Matthew 1:21). In Hebrew, the name means saviour or deliverer, the one who brings freedom and salvation.

In the opening story of Mark 2, a group of companions want to bring a paralysed friend to Jesus while he is in Capernaum (2:1). Such is the crush they cannot get through the door. But they are inventive and bold, and decide to dismantle the roof and lower down their friend on a stretcher to where Jesus stands in the room below. When Jesus sees the man and the faith of his companions, he somewhat surprisingly says, "Son, your sins are forgiven." Some teachers of the law who are present in the house question Jesus's statement, saying: "Why does this fellow talk like that? He's blaspheming! Who can forgive sins but God alone?" (2:6–7). Indeed, only God has authority to forgive sins. In response, Jesus remarks he could just as well say, "Get up, take your mat and walk" (2:9), but he wants to demonstrate that "the Son of Man has authority on earth to forgive sins" (2:10).

There seems to be a triple message here: to the paralysed man, to the teachers of the law and to us as readers of the Gospel. The paralysed man learns that there is a connection between his forgiveness and his healing. We don't know his life story, but it could very well be that his paralysis is in some way connected to either a sinful attitude, such as revenge or bitterness, or some life event for which he is responsible, and that his healing also means acknowledging his guilt. Sickness is by no means always caused by sin (see Job 1:1 or John 9:3) but perhaps in this man there is a very direct link between his physical condition and his lifestyle. With Jesus's words he realizes that not only can he be healed of his paralysis, but his failures have been identified and will be forgiven too. Jesus also demonstrates to the teachers of the law that the Son of Man, Jesus's favourite title for himself, has the authority to forgive sins. This may leave them wondering in their hearts who this Son of Man is. But if they know, and they probably do, they are left with the conclusion that Jesus is claiming divinity, for they too agree that only God has authority to forgive sins (Mark 2:10). Furthermore, when Jesus demonstrates this authority by healing the man (2:12) what more proof do they need? And lastly, for us, the readers of the Gospel, this healing demonstrates not only the authority of Jesus, but also the close connection between healing and forgiveness. Forgiveness received will often bring about a deep release from guilt, but also from a kind of "paralysis" so that our freedom to be truly ourselves is wonderfully restored.

Authority to call disciples (Mark 2:13–17; 3:12–18,20–34)

The second way Jesus reveals his authority in these chapters is through the calling and appointment of apostles. As we have already noted from the first chapter of the Gospel, the calling of a new community, of which the apostles are to be the foundation, is integral to the way Jesus works. They will observe Jesus in action, imitate his example when sent out (Mark 6:1–7), and eventually become the leaders of the new community. Evidently they are slow learners, or sometimes take one step forward and then three steps back, but nonetheless Jesus perseveres with them.

In these verses, Jesus shows his personal authority in calling and appointing the disciples or apostles. The apostles are the twelve to whom are added Matthias after the death of Judas (see Acts 1:12ff.) and the Apostle Paul (1 Corinthians 15:8). These apostles are regarded as having a special and unique authority in the Church (see Ephesians 2:20 and 4:11), which cannot be repeated. And yet they are drawn from lowly backgrounds. As we have seen, four of them are fishermen in Galilee, but are transformed so that the Sanhedrin, the Jewish elite and governors of Jerusalem, while understanding their unschooled background, nevertheless acknowledge their authority as coming from being with Jesus (see Acts 4:13ff.). Nowhere is Jesus's authority in calling apostles clearer than in the call of Levi, or Matthew (2:13–17). A tax collector who mixes with a colourful group of other tax gatherers and is much despised by the Pharisees for working with the Roman authorities, Matthew is nonetheless transfixed by Jesus—so much so that he readily leaves his lucrative profession and "follows" him. In time Matthew becomes the writer of the Gospel of Matthew: the journey Jesus sends him on is from tax gatherer to New Testament author. Nor does Jesus hold on to his authority; he readily transfers some of it to his disciples. Thus, in the appointment of the apostles, we read that their commission is to be with him, to be sent out to preach and to have authority to drive out demons (Mark 3:13–19).

Belonging to this new community will lead to misunderstanding at best and abuse at worst. Jesus's own family do not understand his preoccupation with his task, as they see it, such that he does not even have time to eat (3:20). In exasperation they say, "He is out of his mind," and they try to take charge of him, to place him under their control (3:21). Forgetting what the angel said to her at the time of his conception (Luke 1:26–38), Mary seeks to restrain him and call him home. Jesus will not hear of it: his "mother and brothers" are now those who do the will of his Father (Mark 3:35). This is the new family bond in the new community he is founding: not so much blood-ties as allegiance based on faith. It is a community in which Jesus, the bridegroom, is the centre (2:18–22), in which there is no need for fasting while he is with his disciples, and which is like a new wineskin holding new wine.

The Sabbath

Not only does Jesus demonstrate his authority by forgiving sins, by making exceptional demands of allegiance and sacrifice of his disciples, but perhaps most contentiously, in the eyes of the scribes and Pharisees, he does so by taking charge of the Sabbath.

The Sabbath (Saturday/Shabbat) was one of the fundamental institutions of Judaism, given by Yahweh, the Lord, himself. It symbolized the rest that God had from creation on the seventh day (see Genesis 2:2, 3). It became one of the defining characteristics of Jewish life. But what was in essence a day of blessing for the whole community had become a heavy burden. There were at least three meals shared together on Friday evening, Saturday lunchtime and afternoon that defined the Sabbath. The day was to be one of rest and used to celebrate creation, to remember the Israelite deliverance from Egypt, and as a foretaste of the future. But it had become in the hands of the Pharisees a day bounded by restrictions, to the point where thirty-nine activities were proscribed: from walking long distances to carrying something; from writing and baking to weaving together two threads. In particular, helping others and healing were considered work, and all work was banned.

In this part of the Gospel, there are two actions of Jesus that draw the special criticism of the Pharisees. The first is picking ears of corn when he and his disciples are walking through a field, rubbing the corn in their fingers and extracting the corn to eat from the husk. This action contravenes three of the thirty-nine rules about *melachot* (activities) that are forbidden on the Sabbath: picking, gathering and threshing.

So Jesus is arraigned by the Pharisees. In his defence, he cites a biblical example from the life of David, who, in great hunger, ate the shewbread in the tabernacle (see 1 Samuel 21:1–6). The principle here is surely that human need trumps religious regulation. At the end of his defence, Jesus lays down in a typically pithy and memorable way that "the Sabbath was made for man, not man for the Sabbath" (Mark 2:27). In other words, the day is to be a blessing, not a burden; a celebration, not a labyrinth of rules. And to cap it all, Jesus says, "The Son of Man is Lord even of the Sabbath" (2:28). Once again Jesus is displaying his authority, even over this most sacred Jewish institution.

As if to drive home this authority, Mark immediately follows Jesus's statement with another healing miracle performed on the Sabbath. Indeed, Jesus makes the healing of the man with the withered arm part of his argument that the "Sabbath was made for man". He defiantly calls out to his assembled critics, who are seeking to accuse him. "Which is lawful on the Sabbath: to do good or to do evil, to save life or to kill?" Put like that it is not surprising that "they remained silent" (3:4). But Jesus, knowing their stubborn hearts, is both angry and distressed (3:5). He heals the man who stretches out his withered hand and arm. At this point the Pharisees begin to plot with the Herodians how they might kill Jesus (3:6). If they cannot answer by appealing to their law, they will silence him with force.

This whole episode is a reminder to us that so much of the created world is there for our enjoyment, not to be misused or abused, but well used. The Sabbath is life-giving and life-enhancing. The challenge in our society is finding ways to rest in a truly life-giving way.

Authority over Satan (Mark 3:20–34)

In Jesus's worldview, and indeed that of the Bible, there is an actively malevolent being called Satan. He appears, for instance, in the opening chapter of Job (1:6ff.). Once a most powerful angel who rebelled and was cast down, he now makes the world the place to oppose the increase of God's kingdom and is the one behind the existence of evil in the world.

In the introduction of his book *The Screwtape Letters*, C. S. Lewis writes, "There are two equal and opposite errors into which our race can fall about devils. One is to disbelieve in their existence. The other is to believe, and to feel excessive and unhealthy interest in them. They themselves are equally pleased by both errors and hail a materialist or a magician with the same delight."[6] Jesus has no trouble believing in the existence and the reality of evil spirits and the Devil, although their power is completely circumscribed in his presence. He commands them with a word (Luke 11:20).

Evil spirits can oppress or inhabit an individual, the most notorious example in the Gospel being the Gaderene demoniac (Mark 5:1–20). This man's healing is given a lengthy and detailed description by Mark and is repeated in Matthew and Luke. In John's Gospel, Satan is referred to in one place as a "thief" and in another as a "wolf". John famously wrote, "The thief comes only to steal and kill and destroy; I have come that they may have life, and have it to the full" (John 10:10).

The Pharisees, in casting around for a new line of attack against Jesus, come up with the gross insult that Jesus's authority over evil, and over evil spirits, comes from being himself possessed by Beelzebul—a Jewish name for the prince of devils derived from "Baal", the name for the Canaanite deity. Yet Jesus responds with simple logic and a clear warning. If he is casting out evil spirits by the power of Beelzebul, then Satan's dominion will be split and have little chance of succeeding. Yet if Jesus expels evil spirits by the Holy Spirit, then the kingdom of God is present. Furthermore, if a person wilfully and persistently calls the work of the Holy Spirit the work of Satan, then he or she commits a sin so great that it is unforgivable (Mark 3:29).

In these two chapters, Mark demonstrates the authority of Jesus: his authority to forgive sins, his authority in calling disciples like Matthew and the other apostles, his authority over the Sabbath, and finally his authority over evil and the evil one.

Jesus's authority was markedly different from other forms of authority that Mark had witnessed. The crowds themselves had remarked that Jesus's authority was different and "new" compared with the Pharisees (1:22, 27). Mark must also have reflected, when living in Rome, and when compiling and even writing his Gospel, how different Jesus's authority was from the form of authority exercised there. It is not beyond the realms of possibility that Mark would have seen the Emperor making his way through the streets of the city, surrounded by the Praetorian guard. Nero's authority was based on force and fear. By contrast Jesus's authority was based on liberating people from their greatest burdens: granting forgiveness, giving meaning and purpose to life, providing true rest, and liberating those oppressed by evil. It was undoubtedly a whole new form of authority. And it was in entering the kingdom of the beloved Son that this freedom was to be found.

CHAPTER 3

Growth and Secrecy

Mark 4:1–34

There is a tension at the heart of Mark's message between openness and secrecy. How might a campaign manager be regarded by his party or by a leader seeking re-election, if he were to say, "We are trying to keep your identity and ability a secret. We are *not* going to broadcast any stories about the people you have helped or healed. We are *not* going on air with advertisements extolling your skills, your ability or your future programme. No, we are telling people as little as possible during your lifetime. Furthermore, if pressed, we will tell stories we will call parables or allegories. Our vision for the future will 'germinate' in those who think hard about them. At the same time, your strategy will remain hidden from those who want easy answers. We reckon in this way we can grow our base from about a dozen firm followers to several billion over time"?

The would-be president might well say, "Pull the other one, it's got bells on!" and then sack that campaign manager and look for another one.

And yet this is the way Jesus proceeds. He is concerned about growth, but not in the way that almost all worldly movements bring about growth. He does in fact want his actions and identity to remain a secret!

The kingdom and growth

All living organisms grow. If they don't grow, they die. All empires have sought to grow also, normally by force and acquisition. This was true of the Roman Empire, which used immense force to occupy and colonize Europe. In conquering Gaul, it is said that Julius Caesar killed a million Gauls. Indeed, one of the most moving pieces of sculpture in the Capitoline Museum in Rome is *The Dying Gaul*, which, although believed to be of a Gaul from Galatia, could very well represent the thousands killed in Gaul by Rome. Human kingdoms advance through war, but God's kingdom advances through the *word*, by winning the hearts and minds of people.

The parables that follow in swift succession in Chapter 4 of Mark's Gospel tell us of the nature of this growth. Jesus uses parables to describe growth in the kingdom and to reveal what the kingdom is like. The use of parables is nevertheless much more circumscribed in Mark than in Luke and Matthew. It seems that Luke and Matthew relished their inclusion. Luke gives us uniquely the Parable of the Prodigal Son (Luke 15:11–32, perhaps the greatest parable of all) and the Parable of the Good Samaritan (Luke 10:25ff.), while Matthew alone gives us the Parable of the Sheep and the Goats, which underscores the disciples' responsibility (Matthew 25:31ff.). For his part, Mark limits himself to very few parables, most of which are found in Chapter 4 and are about the growth of the kingdom. It seems that Mark prefers the breathless narrative—hence the frequent use of the word "immediately" concerning Jesus's actions—to the long discourses of John and the extended teaching and parables of Matthew and Luke (as in the Sermon on the Mount and Plain respectively).

However, Mark gives us the *raison d'etre* of the parables, which touches on the theme of secrecy and hiddenness. Following the telling of the Parable of the Sower, the meaning of which we will return to, the disciples ask Jesus for an interpretation. Jesus prefaces his explanation with an important prologue, saying: "The secret of the kingdom of God has been given to you. But to those on the outside everything is said in parables" (Mark 4:11). Then Jesus quotes an enigmatic verse from Isaiah, in which it is said, the purpose of parables is so that "they may be ever seeing but never perceiving, and ever hearing but never understanding; otherwise they might turn and be forgiven" (Mark 4:12; Isaiah 6:9–10). At face value, one might say that Jesus tells parables in order that the truth will be hidden or obfuscated, so that people will not repent and be forgiven. In other words, parables can be seen as a deliberate camouflaging of the truth to prevent understanding. But that would be absurd and would contradict the rest of Scripture, which desires that all people be saved (see 1 Timothy 2:4). It could mean, however, that the parable acts as a kind of spiritual sieve.

Sieves are at the forefront of my mind at the time of writing as we are sieving the compost to separate stones and larger twigs from the enriching matter. Most of the composted earth goes through. In the same way, a parable demands responsible listening by the hearer, hence Jesus's saying: "He who has ears to hear, let him hear" (Mark 4:9). Hearing, in the Jewish sense, means listening and acting in accordance with perceived truth. Thus a parable will have the effect of sifting the spiritual intent of the hearer, with the result that some will not perceive, some will not understand and so some will not turn and be forgiven. Others will. Attentive hearing will be rewarded, but those who cannot be bothered, or who have declined any form of spiritual quest from the outset, will not be rewarded.

The Parable of the Sower is about growth, although it seems a wasteful and inefficient way of growth. I am sure many could arrange for a better method, but those were the techniques of the day and, as such, influenced Jesus's thinking about the sowing of God's word.

There are four types of soil on which the seed of God's word or message alights, and with very varying results. The seed lying on the path is rootless and an easy target for Satan, who pecks it up like a hungry bird. The seed in rocky places initially does well, and is received with joy (Mark 4:16), but it also has no root, so that when times become difficult, it "quickly falls away". The third type of soil is infested with weeds and the seed struggles for space to grow. So too the word in some people is choked; it is overcome by the worries of life, the deceitfulness of riches and the desire for material things.

The final soil is good, and the seed is very fruitful, bearing thirty, sixty or a hundred times what is sown. What is clear is that for the seed to grow in such soil, there needs to be both a *good root structure* and *space to develop*. This equates in human life to having a real understanding in both heart and mind of the message of the kingdom of God and space to develop the priorities of the kingdom. If these are in short supply, long-term growth and fruitfulness will be well-nigh impossible.

Jesus's Parable of the Sower or the Soils is fulfilled countless times, for the spiritual struggle it represents remains the same in every generation.

Yet equally, the fruitfulness of the few assures the overall growth of the kingdom.

The two other parables about growth in Mark's sequence are the Parable of the Growing Seed (4:26–29) and the Parable of the Mustard Seed (4:30–32). The former highlights that the silent growth of the seed is like that of the word. It is noiseless, it is continuous, it is fruitful. In these respects, it is so like plant life. I enjoy growing vegetables. It is wonderfully satisfying to harvest potatoes, say. You plant them in spring and from July onwards they are ready to harvest—five, six or more healthy potatoes from a single seed potato. They have been growing silently, continuously and fruitfully all the while. The miracle of growth enabled by the genes of the potato, the soil, the sun and the rain is always awesome. Likewise, the seed of God's message can, as in the good soil of the sower, produce remarkable results. I am reminded of a man who heard singing, came into our church, in time became a youth worker, and has produced videos encouraging young people in their faith almost every day of the COVID-19 pandemic.

The second of the two short growth parables in this chapter is that of the mustard seed (4:30–32). The essence of this parable is that from very small beginnings great results can sprout. The mustard shrub may not be the largest tree, but it was often the largest shrub in the kitchen garden of a Jewish home. It frequently amazes me just how large a plant or tree can become from the smallest seed. This year there are literally hundreds of acorns from the oak tree in our garden. If they all grew to the size of their parent, there would be a mighty forest. The kingdom of God may start from the tiniest beginnings, but it has the potential to grow to a very significant size. This is true of the kingdom of God overall, but it is also true of all its manifestations in its many particular locations.

Secrecy and revelation

While there is the promise of a great harvest or growth contained in this message about the kingdom of God, this growth will come about in an unexpected way: subtly, steadfastly, irresistibly and profoundly. In other words, the growth of the kingdom and the healing of an individual come not through dazzlement, but by being drawn into relationship; not by being dumbfounded, but by being convinced; not by witnessing spectacular things, but by understanding essential truth. What does this mean?

Whenever Jesus performed a miracle of healing on an individual, he called for secrecy. Why was that? Because he was diffident about his power and authority? Because it was a form of crowd control—else he would be overwhelmed by numbers? Possibly (see Mark 1:45b). Frequently, he enjoined secrecy and even silence on those who were transformed (see 1:44; 3:12; 7:36; 8:26). Only the restored Gaderene demoniac is encouraged to go home and tell those who know him (5:19). The point may be that Jesus did not want people to make up their minds about him in the way they might about a charismatic healer, or a peripatetic exorcist, or a fashionable rabbi—of which there were many in first century Palestine. No, he wanted people to respond to the totality of his story: his example, his demeanour, his simplicity, his teaching with authority, his compassionate action in miracles, his courage, his difference from the Pharisees, his crucifixion and what it meant, and finally his resurrection. He wanted no flash-in-the-pan following, but a deep and steady burn resulting from complete trust in him as Messiah and Son of God. To understand this was to understand the true secret (4:11, 34b), and by being secretive about his acts of power Jesus hoped to focus attention on the deeper reality of who he truly was.

Jesus would frequently explain the nature of his Messiahship to his disciples, but just as frequently they did not understand it, especially when he told them that he would be killed after being rejected by the elders, the chief priests and the teachers of the law (8:31). The Messianic secret was his identity: laid bare by Mark at the outset of his Gospel where he announced it was all about Jesus the Messiah and the Son of God (1:1). Yet Jesus did not openly state this until asked by the High Priest, "'Are you the Messiah, the Son of the Blessed One?' 'I am,' said Jesus. 'And you will see the Son of Man sitting at the right hand of the Mighty One, and coming on the clouds of heaven'" (14:61b–62). At this the High Priest tore his clothes, because it was blasphemous if it were not true (14:63, 64).

There is a time for secrecy and a time for telling. Once again Jesus sets the timetable. He tells the disciples after the Transfiguration not to tell anyone what they have seen "until the Son of Man [has] risen from the dead" (9:9). Likewise, Jesus tells his disciples in Mark 4, "Whatever is hidden is meant to be disclosed, and whatever is concealed is meant to be brought out into the open" (4:22). After the resurrection, the secret is out of the bag, the time for concealment and secrecy is over. His disciples are to go into all the world and make disciples.

What is clear from these verses in Chapter 4 is that God's reign, God's kingdom, will grow. There will be waste, but growth is assured. This growth will not come about through brash advertising, through vaunting of power, or through the use of force. Instead, it will be almost self-effacing. Like the seed beneath the ground, it will be unseen, but it will be unstoppable. Like a plant that breaks through concrete, the kingdom will break through the hardest places. And how unlike the spread of human kingdoms and powers this will be, with their requirement for armies, generals, brutal force, intimidation, executions.

Perhaps as Mark's thumb moved over the Roman coin in his toga pocket, he knew once again how different this kingdom of the Messiah was from the one proclaimed by Emperor Nero. Now he would write about the signs of this kingdom and the power of this secret king.

CHAPTER 4

Signs of the Kingdom and the King

Mark 4:35–6:56

In this chapter, we come to the central part of Jesus's ministry around Galilee. The section divides into three parts: Jesus's ministry over the natural created world; Jesus's ministry of restoration through healing and deliverance, which is emulated by the apostles in their mission; and the shadow of the cross anticipated by the execution of John the Baptist. In this way Mark demonstrates the quality of the kingdom rule of Jesus and the opposition it finds in the world.

Jesus's rule over creation

Never have we been better informed about the challenges to the created order than we are today. The issues that threaten the health of the planet and its manifold life are these: climate change; destruction of forests; an increase in human population from three to six billion in fifty years; the unceasing poaching of great animals; the trafficking of animals such as pangolins; the destruction of habitats and biodiversity; over-fishing of the seas by industrial trawling; the wastage of food (we throw away 40 per cent); and the accumulation of waste, including plastic, in our seas and lands. By comparison, two thousand years ago in Palestine, the created order was pristine.

The ministry of Jesus around Galilee recorded by Mark shows him responding to the needs of men and women, as well as demonstrating that he is lord of all creation. Mark does not draw out the theology of Christ's divine power over creation in the way that Paul does in his writings (especially Romans 8), or as John does in the Prologue to his Gospel. Famously, in Colossians Paul teaches this pre-eminence of Christ, writing: "For by him all things were created: things in heaven and on earth, visible and invisible, whether thrones or powers or authorities: all things were created by him and for him. He is before all things, and in him all things hold together" (1:15–17). In fact, Paul most probably wrote this letter before the time of Mark's Gospel, extolling Christ's supremacy over both creation and the Church. Some thirty years later, the Apostle John wrote his Gospel, most probably in Ephesus. Like Paul, John was seeking to hold together Christ's authority over the material and the spiritual realms, at a time when, with the advent of Gnosticism, some teachers wanted to denigrate the significance of the flesh and the material world by saying that Jesus did not really come in the flesh. Thus John writes, "Through him all things were made; without him nothing was made that has been made. In him was life, and that life was the light of all mankind" (John 1:3, 4). In effect, John is saying that everything in creation has the stamp of the creator. Just as silver bears the hallmark of its maker, giving it greater value, so too creation in all its parts is a witness to its original creator. Jesus's ministry in Galilee demonstrates this.

There are three miracles that demonstrate this lordship over creation. They are the Calming of the Storm (Mark 4:35–41), the Feeding of the Five Thousand (6:30–44) and Jesus Walking on Water (6:45–56). They are all miracles or signs of authority over the natural world.

I often reflect how reduced the canvas would have been for Jesus's ministry had there been no Lake Galilee. There would have been no stilling of the storm, no potential for danger ("Don't you care if we drown?"), no walking on water, no faith gymnasium for the disciples, no opportunity to give the crowds the slip, no great catch of fish, no fishing metaphors for evangelism, and no barbecue on the beach, as described by John in Chapter 21 of his Gospel. All these moments were opportunities for Jesus to demonstrate his authority, to train the disciples, and provide a backdrop for worship and understanding who he really was. Anyone visiting Galilee today will recognize that its very serenity is an invitation to prayer and contemplation, just as its storms still herald a need for faith (Mark 4:40).

The stilling of the storm is a timeless demonstration of Jesus's power: it is both miracle and parable, as often the signs of the kingdom are (e.g., the turning of water into wine in John 2). The story is delightfully full of eyewitness detail that must have come from Peter. They go across the lake at Jesus's instigation. They take him "just as he is", for presumably he has made no provision for extra clothing for the journey. He sleeps in the stern, peacefully and deeply! His head is on a "cushion". And then the storm comes: fast, furious, frightening and dangerous. Jesus continues sleeping; the disciples are provoked into crying out, "Teacher, don't you care if we drown?" (4:38). He stills the storm with a word, addressing the wind as if it is a sentient being: "Quiet! Be still" (4:39). It becomes completely calm. He then gently rebukes not the wind, but the turmoil in the hearts of the disciples. "Why are you so afraid? Do you still have no faith?" (4:40). The "still" is a little humbling; it means that despite being with Jesus for a little while, their faith score has not improved! The sudden stilling of the storm gives way to the question, asked in some awe: "Who is this? Even the wind and the waves obey him" (4:41). It is clear proof that he the creator has authority over the creation.

I have sometimes spoken on the storms of the Bible and what they teach us. Jonah, for example, is responsible for a storm of his own making, for he runs away from the will of God when he is commanded to go and preach to the people of Nineveh. As an orthodox Jew, he prefers not to go to Nineveh, especially if God is going to forgive these "unwashed" Gentiles (see Jonah 1:1–6; 4:1–3). The Apostle Paul encounters a fierce storm on the way to Jerusalem, but through it is able to take the Gospel to Malta, its governor and people (Acts 27:13–28:10). And here in this account of a storm on Galilee, Jesus accompanies his disciples throughout, rebukes their lack of faith and brings peace in the midst of it. Thus storms in life may be of our own making, come during the course of mission, or arise when we are following his command (see Mark 4:35). The lesson from this miracle, which teaches a spiritual truth much like a parable, is that faith is never out of place in life's stormy weather, and that peace may be found even in the midst of a storm.

The second of the three nature miracles in these chapters is the Feeding of the Five Thousand. So familiar to us, it nonetheless teaches us an immensely important truth about Jesus's rule. It has the same ring to it as the turning of water into wine (John 2): sumptuous provision from limited resources. In the case of the wedding at Cana, it was turning water into excellent wine. Here it is the multiplication of five loaves and two fish into sufficient food for five thousand men (and presumably many children and women too, although not counted!). It is an extraordinary miracle of divine provision.

Not only that, but the miracle is couched in terms that will train the disciples and has deep symbolism. Once again it is a miracle that not only feeds but teaches. It teaches the disciples that they can expect Jesus to multiply resources. It anticipates the Last Supper with its similar actions: Jesus takes what is offered by the people, gives thanks, breaks the loaves and distributes them through his disciples (see Mark 14:22–25). Presumably it is as the bread and fish are distributed that they do not run out. They simply go on being multiplied. And in the end, the final symbol: twelve baskets are gathered. Surely enough for all Israel should they desire Jesus's bread.

The last nature miracle in this section is Jesus Walking on the Water. Like the other two, it is both a miracle and also a symbol or parable. The miracle of walking on water is a supernatural way of reaching the disciples, his companions, as they struggle to row around the lake to Bethsaida (6:45). Having stayed behind on the mountainside, Jesus decides to go to them. Not having a boat, he walks on water. In Mark's Gospel, we are not told of Peter's attempt to walk on water, which is surprising, since Peter is the source of most of the stories of Jesus's ministry. Perhaps Mark is sparing Peter's blushes. Jesus gives the impression that Peter could have walked on water had he not taken his eyes off him and looked instead at the wind and the waves (Matthew 14:27–31). The effect on the disciples in the two versions is also quite different: Mark tells us the disciples do not understand because "their hearts [are] hardened" (Mark 6:52); Matthew tells us those in the boat worship him and say, "Truly you are the Son of God" (Matthew 14:33). It is hard to reconcile the responses.

Yet alongside the miracle there is a further symbolic point. Jesus is literally above his creation. In other words, Jesus is always distinct from the created order. Idolatry is the worship of something created: a crocodile, the sun, an egret, a wooden pole, an image. If that all seems rather outdated today, we may worship a political theory, an iPhone, food and drink, our bodies, sex, or a certain lifestyle. The prophets continually indicted Israel on the grounds that they "have forsaken me, the spring of living water, and have dug their own cisterns, broken cisterns that cannot hold water" (Jeremiah 2:13; Psalm 115). Jesus is to be worshipped as distinct from creation, and that will become lifegiving.

In these three miracles, Jesus demonstrates his sovereignty over creation: wind, food and water. He will also show that he is lord over sickness, evil and death.

Jesus's rule over human life

Jesus's Galilean ministry exemplified three types of healing: the freeing of a man from demonic infestation, the healing of a woman with a perennial illness, and the raising of a child from the dead. Together they showcase the nature of the kingdom of God, and the rule that Jesus is bringing.

The healing of the Gadarene demoniac (Mark 5:1–20) has to be one of the most extreme examples of deliverance in the whole of the New Testament. The sheer scale of the possession of this man by a legion of evil spirits is both disturbing and distressing.

The symptoms of his demonization are all too evident: he lives among the tombs, displaying superhuman and frightening strength, crying out and defying normal human interactions and self-harming by cutting himself (5:1–5). He is an isolated figure robbed of all normal humanity, beyond the care of the local population. Jesus steps ashore and, like a magnet, the demoniac is drawn to him (5:2, 6), shouting, "What do you want with me, Jesus, Son of the Most High God?" (5:7). While others, including his disciples, are hard pushed to truly identify him, the evil spirit, by contrast, with its evil genius knows exactly who Jesus is. Jesus addresses the evil spirit by asking who it is. The response comes: "My name is Legion, for we are many" (5:9). Knowing the names of the spirits is the first step in exercising control over them. They have no choice but to obey Jesus's command and, knowing this, they ask to inhabit other creatures, the pigs. Why they should be granted their request given the destruction they will cause is hard to fathom, but the extent of their evil influence is evident when the whole herd of swine (unclean creatures to the Jews) is sent headlong into the sea.

The man is left quiet, clothed and in his right mind, with his ordeal at an end and wanting thereafter to be with Jesus. The local population is disturbed by the loss to their livelihood, and the great power that has been displayed (5:14–17). They want Jesus to leave, whereas the healed demoniac would like to stay close to his liberator. He is told to go home to the Decapolis and tell his family and friends what has happened to him. The Decapolis was southern Syria, probably a Gentile region, and outside the boundaries of Israel. He will thus become a missionary to an area as yet untouched by Jesus's ministry. Meanwhile, Jesus crosses back to the west side of the lake in the region of Capernaum, to further display the power of his rule.

So much of Jesus's ministry occurs "on the way": sometimes it is his teaching that is given *en route* to another place, sometimes he heals a person he meets along the way. This idea of Jesus teaching and healing whilst walking around Galilee gives immediacy and dynamic momentum to his ministry, and no doubt accounts for Mark's frequent use of the word "immediately". No miracle is more "on the way" nor more immediate than the healing of the woman with the flow of blood, however (5:24–34; see also Acts 10:37–38).

The context of this healing is that it is set within another. Jairus, an eminent man in the community and a synagogue ruler (perhaps like a patron of a parish church), flings himself at Jesus's feet, beseeching him to come to his daughter, who is dying. Jesus goes with him to his house, and "on the way" a woman who has suffered from a flow of blood for twelve years, and who has spent all her money on doctors, debates within herself whether to touch Jesus, believing she will be healed (5:28). She does so, and immediately her bleeding stops (5:29). Because of the ostracism she suffers from society due to Jewish ritual laws (Leviticus 15:25–30), and because of the delicacy of her complaint, she seeks healing in secret. Yet Jesus, sensing "power [has] gone out of him", wants the woman to know not only physical restoration, but through an authoritative word from him, be restored in the community and healed from all feelings of low self-esteem. Having stopped, he says: "Who touched me?" The woman comes forward and with words of comfort Jesus confirms her healing and gives his blessing of peace (5:34).

All this happens on the way to Jairus's house, but almost as soon as Jesus says to the woman who has touched him, "Daughter, your faith has healed you", Jairus hears from his servants that *his* daughter has died. Aware of Jairus's shock, Jesus says, "Don't be afraid; just believe" (5:36)—surely one of the great mottos of the Gospel.

On entering the home of Jairus, Jesus takes in only Peter, James and John, the inner circle of disciples. He gets rid of all the professional mourners, calling the girl's death "sleep", and bids her rise (5:41). And "immediately" the girl stands up and walks around. Practical, as with the gathering up of remnant food at the Feeding of the Five Thousand, Jesus asks the astonished family to give her food but also enjoins secrecy! What hope was there of that! (5:43).

The cost of the kingdom

If the rule of Jesus brought healing and freedom to a whole range of individuals afflicted with sickness, evil spirits or even death, it did not come without cost. Alongside the stories of the healing of the Gadarene demoniac, the restoration to life of Jairus's daughter, and the healing of the woman with the flow of blood, is the account of John the Baptist's execution (Mark 6:14–29), and the refusal of people to recognize Jesus for who he really was in his hometown of Nazareth. There was a cost in terms of human approval and acceptance in bringing in this kingdom.

Nowhere is this more acute than in the treatment of John the Baptist. This fearless figure calls for a new spiritual beginning through the gateway of repentance and baptism, for forgiveness of sins. Not only does John call people to Jordan's river for baptism, but he is also unreserved in pointing out the obligations of different groups of people: those with enough should share their surplus, tax collectors should levy no more than their due, and soldiers should not extort money through intimidation (Luke 3:7ff.). Nor are rulers beyond his criticism: Herod the Tetrarch, one of the sons of Herod the Great, is censured for divorcing his first wife and marrying Herodias, his sister-in-law, who deeply resents this intervention in her personal life. Given the opportunity to get rid of John the Baptist, she takes it in the most vindictive and shocking way. Her daughter Salome dances beautifully on Herod's birthday. To please his guests and display his princely power, he rashly promises anything she might ask, up to half his kingdom. When she is instructed by her mother to ask for John the Baptist's head on a platter, there is shock and consternation, particularly from Herod, who likes listening to John (Mark 6:20b). The grisly execution is performed in John's cell, and his head is brought on a platter to Herod. If artists like Caravaggio have made much of the egregious theatre of the moment, as in his painting which hangs in the Co-Cathedral of St John in Valetta, the capital of Malta, such artworks cannot disguise the cost of John's calling, to be "a voice of one calling in the wilderness, 'Prepare the way for the Lord'" (1:3). Jesus's kingdom is heralded by events of healing and freedom, but also meets deep opposition, vindictiveness and self-serving ambition. News of John's death no doubt casts a shadow across Jesus's path, reminding him of the trials and suffering that await him.

If the persecution of John the Baptist is cruel, shocking and deeply malicious, the opposition to Jesus in his hometown of Nazareth is sullen, grudging and grumpy. Where does he get his wisdom? How is it this carpenter can fix bodies and not just wood? Isn't he the eldest of a large family of at least seven children from the town (6:3)? Their very familiarity with Jesus limits their ability to receive. As they have little expectation, they have little to show for Jesus's presence with them. Jesus makes the telling remark that in his own family, among his own relatives and townspeople, a prophet is without honour (6:4). Indeed, "he could not do any miracles there, except lay his hands on a few people who were ill and heal them" (6:5). There is mutual amazement: they at the authority, reputation and wisdom of this Nazarene, whom they can only regard as the "boy down the road", and he at their lack of faith (compare 6:2 with 6:6).

The apostles have a better story to tell on their return from mission (6:12). One way or another the kingdom that Jesus is bringing will take root. But the response to his presence and work will never be uniform.

CHAPTER 5

Responses to Jesus

Mark 7:1–8:26

In this section we see the full range of responses to the work, words and presence of Jesus. In keeping with the Gospels generally, it is those with the least claim to understand who have the greatest grasp of the truth of Jesus's power. In these verses, we see the blindness and superficiality of the Pharisees, and the dullness of the disciples, versus the acuity of the Syrophoenician woman and the amazement of the crowds. Those who should recognize him do not; those who have maximum exposure to him fail to understand, and a woman who is well outside the household of faith, whether Pharisee or disciple, grasps *exactly* what Jesus is able to do and presumably who he is. It is one more case of the first being last, and the last being first.

The Pharisees are shocked. Indeed they make a habit of being shocked and would have surprised themselves if they had not been. This occasion for being shocked is not about observance or non-observance of the Sabbath (Mark 2:24), or about pronouncing forgiveness when only God can forgive (2:10). No, they have come down from Jerusalem (7:1) most likely to gather further evidence for their indictment of this rabbi, who, to their minds, is quite out of order. And this time *it is all about washing.* This is the perfect opportunity to show how Jesus breaks their traditions, but for Jesus it is the perfect opportunity to teach what is wrong with the human family.

Washing is a distinguishing feature of Judaism. On one level it is highly sensible to wash hands before a meal, but Mark is here observing that the disciples are not washing their hands *ritually*, according to "the tradition of the elders" (7:3). This type of washing, probably much more elaborate, is what the disciples are seemingly neglecting. At root, the Pharisees object to the failure of Jesus's disciples to adhere to the traditions expected of a Jew, and more especially of a rabbi and his disciples. The dispute quickly widens into a debate about the Pharisees' observation of traditions, rather than the commands of God, i.e., Scripture.

Jesus applies these words of Isaiah to the Pharisees: "These people honour me with their lips, but their hearts are far from me. They worship me in vain; their teachings are merely human rules" (7:6b–7 and Isaiah 29:13). He then gives an example of how this happens in practice, when the Pharisees insist on people giving money set aside as an offering (*korban*) to the synagogue or temple, perhaps the result of a rash vow, rather than supporting their parents. In this instance, a tradition prevents a person from fulfilling their lawful duty to their parents, and from complying with the Fifth Commandment (Exodus 20:12). Putting tradition before the commandment is Jesus's complaint; but even more than that, there is a fundamental underlying issue to be teased out.

In fact, the spirituality of the Pharisees is all wrong. Jesus puts it in a typically pithy way: "Nothing outside a person can defile them by going into them. Rather, it is *what comes out of a person that defiles them*" (Mark 7:15). Mark recognizes the implications of this, for he adds tellingly (7:19b) that by this Jesus declares all foods clean, and overturns centuries of avoidance of prohibited food (see Leviticus 11 and Acts 10:15, 16). The Pharisees are obsessed with cleaning the outside, while Jesus says that nothing but a deep clean of the heart will do.

Taking his disciples to one side, Jesus makes this abundantly clear. It is the heart that must be cleansed, not just the hands, for out of the heart comes "sexual immorality, theft, murder, adultery, greed, malice, deceit, lewdness, envy, slander, arrogance and folly" (7:21b–22). The heart is a great manufacturer of evil, or as the saying goes, "the heart of the human problem is the problem of the human heart". This is Jesus's diagnosis. Handwashing (although important, and no more so than when confronted by a deadly virus), or hand-wringing, will not do—heart change is what is needed.

It is this diagnosis of the human condition that is of the essence of Christianity. It is sobering, unflattering and realistic, and it parts company with other diagnoses of the human condition. Communism believes that if you change the economic conditions of the human race, you will ameliorate its lot, but invariably the common ownership of property leads to dictatorship. Pelagianism, a heresy stemming from the fourth-century heresiarch Pelagius, believed that humans were essentially good and capable of reaching salvation by themselves. By contrast, Christianity acknowledges that although all humans are made in the image of God and capable of acts of great goodness, immense altruism, self-sacrifice and kindness, nevertheless we are all tainted, *incurvatus se* (curved in on ourselves, as Luther said), and flawed. Because of this we need redemption, unmerited forgiveness and grace. We can never attain salvation by trying to keep the rules, for we will surely fall short.

While the Pharisees' reaction to Jesus was that he was breaking tradition and teaching his disciples to do so too, it had the effect of drawing from Jesus a profound and vital insight into the state of the human soul.

The Syrophoenician Woman (Mark 7:24–30)

Mark must have known that he was putting two utterly contrasting reactions to Jesus next to each other in his Gospel: that of the Pharisees and that of the Syrophoenician woman. The former were soaked in the traditions of Judaism, immersed in the Jewish Law or Torah, while the Syrophoenician woman was not a Jew, but a Greek living in Tyre, an ancient city in present-day Lebanon. She is one of a number of feisty individuals in the Gospels, not always known for the virtue of their lives, but for the frankness of their speech. Others include the woman at the well (John 4), the centurion (Luke 7:1–10), and the man born blind (John 9:1–34).

In this story, which Peter would have remembered clearly, Jesus retreats to an area north of Israel on the coast of Phoenicia near Tyre or Sidon, perhaps to find the rest and relaxation he had wanted to give the disciples earlier (see Mark 6:31). In any event, he is recognized by this woman, who it seems has pieced together the stories she has heard about Jesus and discovered the presence in her town of this man with his twelve disciples. Jesus wants secrecy, but his cover is blown (7:24). She begs

Jesus to dispel an evil spirit from her daughter (7:25, 26), but Jesus seems reluctant to help, either because he genuinely thinks his ministry is to be confined to Israel—although he has already helped many Gentiles—or because he believes his reluctance will draw out this woman's desire and faith. Either way, Jesus's response to her request for help—"It is not right to take the children's bread and toss it to the dogs" (7:27)—is on the face of it off-putting at best and discriminatory at worst. Yet so determined and feisty is the woman that she presses on with her plea with wit, verve and faith. "Lord . . . even the dogs under the table eat the children's crumbs" (7:28), she responds. For such a reply her daughter is healed.

There is no doubt that the wholehearted response of this woman is also a rebuke to the Pharisees. After all, they know the privileges of Israel, of which there are many (see Romans 9:4–5; 3:1, 2; 3:27–31), but choose out of ignorance to find fault with the Messiah (Mark 1:1). This woman knows little of these privileges (Romans 9:4–5) but justified by faith (Romans 3:29–31), believes in the Messiah and finds life in his name. If the Pharisees and the Syrophoenician woman are at opposite ends of the poles of faith, oscillating somewhere in the middle are the slow-witted and dull disciples.

The response of the disciples

The response of the disciples revolves around the Feeding of the Four Thousand. There seems more than a touch of *déjà vu* to this account, not that that makes it any the less astonishing, but they do not seem to have learnt any faith-lessons from the Feeding of the Five Thousand.

Once again, a large crowd surrounds Jesus, listening to his teaching. Whatever food they had has been used up, as they have already been with him three days (Mark 8:2). As before, Jesus has compassion for them (8:2 and 6:34). Despite the previous miraculous feeding of the five thousand, the disciples are foxed as to what they might do! They realize it is a remote place, with no likelihood of procuring food. But this time they identify seven loaves and later some fish. Once again Jesus gets the crowd to sit down, and they are fed from seven loaves and a few fish, and seven baskets of leftovers are picked up at the end.

If, as we shall see, the disciples are slow learners, the Pharisees reveal themselves entirely blinkered by their own worldview, and, after the feeding of four thousand, have the temerity to "ask for a sign" (8:11)! As a group, the Pharisees have seen any number of signs, some of which they have objected to (2:12). Now, despite what they have seen in front of their eyes, they ask for a further sign. No wonder Jesus sighs (8:12). Jesus responds that no further sign shall be given them and, in an extended response recorded in Matthew, says the only sign given to this generation will be the sign of Jonah (Matthew 12:38ff.), who was in the belly of the fish for three days, just as the Son of Man will be in the belly of the earth before his resurrection.

Jesus is only a little less exasperated by the spiritual slow-wittedness of his disciples. Slow to respond to the needs of the four thousand in a way that reveals they have not learnt the lesson of the Feeding of the Five Thousand, they now begin fussing in the boat that they have forgotten the bread. Ignoring their oversight, Jesus uses the theme of bread to draw out a lesson about the "the yeast of the Pharisees and Herod" (Mark 8:15). After all, the former were seeking to kill Jesus, while Herod had just overseen the execution of John the Baptist at the whim of his illicit wife, Herodias. Yet such is the literal and prosaic mindset of the disciples, they think Jesus's allusion to yeast is because they have failed to bring any bread on the sea crossing to Dalmanutha (8:9, 10). Aware of this, Jesus abandons his attempt to explain the reference to the yeast of the Pharisees and Herod, and instead concentrates on getting them to understand the implications of feeding so many with so little, and of having so much left over. Indeed, never have so many been fed by so little.

Not only are the responses of the disciples slow, especially compared to the sharp awareness the Syrophoenician woman has of Jesus's ability to heal, but the turgid reactions of the disciples and the antipathy of the Pharisees seem to be reflected also in the somewhat laboured healing of a blind man at Bethsaida—a man who needs a second touch to restore his sight fully (8:24–26)—and the healing of the deaf mute (7:31–35), whose recovery requires more than a word.

If the disciples are proving to be slow learners, their entire expectation of the Messiah is about to be radically reset in light of what he has come to do. This will be the most challenging truth they will face. It will also be the most revolutionary exhibition of kingly power through an abdication of all power in a humiliating death. And in this insight we come to the heart of the Gospel.

CHAPTER 6

The Turning at the Crossroads

Mark 8:27–9:32

Ask an historian to come up with turning points in history, and they might mention 1914, 1918, 1939 and 1945. Likewise, 2016 was a turning point for the UK in deciding to leave the European Union, while the coronavirus pandemic of 2020 will prove to be a global turning point in many ways. We will look at life differently as a result. Other turning points were ushered in by scientific change: the combustion engine, air travel, electricity, radio communications, the pill, and, in my lifetime, the worldwide web and digital communication. In this passage we come to the greatest turning point in Jesus's ministry, a crossroads indeed.

Jesus very deliberately takes his disciples aside by going to Caesarea Philippi, not far from the slopes of Mount Hermon in northern Israel, in the present-day Golan Heights region, and close to a shrine to the Greek god Pan. Perhaps there is an irony here, in that Jesus is to reveal himself here as the true Lord and Messiah from which would come his Greek title of *Pantocrator*, meaning all powerful. Having reached this out-of-the-way place at the edge of Syria, Jesus asks his disciples to identify him. He does this by asking them a question in two phases: "Who do *people* say I am?" (Mark 8:27) and then, "Who do *you* say that I am?" (8:29). The first question elicits the general response that some say he is John the Baptist, presumably somehow returned to life, that others say Elijah, whose return is expected by Jews, and that still others believe he is another of the prophets. Then Jesus presses the question, making it more personal, with "Who do you say I am?" It is a probing question concerning his identity, and the answer must be based on the evidence that the disciples have seen in the last few months of Jesus's Galilean ministry.

Peter replies that Jesus is the Christ, the Anointed One or Messiah. Although this is true—as Jesus tells Peter in the longer version of this story given in Matthew 16:13ff. (in which Peter is credited with this revelation having been given to him by the Father)—it does not indicate what Jesus will *do* as Messiah, since there were many beliefs in Judaism concerning the Messiah's role: he was to be like the priests and kings of Israel in the Old Testament, who were anointed with oil (e.g., Exodus 29:7, 21; 1 Samuel 10:1), or he was to be like Cyrus (Isaiah 45:1), anointed to deliver Israel from exile in Persia. But more recently in the life of Israel, since the Maccabees of 164 BC, there was a burning hope that the Messiah or Anointed One would come soon to deliver Israel from occupation by foreign powers and, in particular, the Romans. If Peter has correctly identified Jesus as Messiah, under the guidance of the Spirit, he is now to learn how this Anointed One will bring liberation to Israel and the world. Indeed, all the false assumptions of Peter and the other disciples will gradually be blown away, and completely recrafted, but it will take some time to change their false expectations.

The crossroads

In keeping with the general tenor of Mark's Gospel, the conversation moves swiftly on. In response to Peter's correct identification of Jesus as Messiah, Jesus immediately fills in the substance of this role, that is, he describes the true vocation of the Messiah: "He [the Messiah] must be killed and after three days rise again" (Mark 8:31). It is clear that more is said about this than we have here, which is a summary, for we are told "he spoke plainly about this" (8:32).

Peter's immediate response is to disbelieve what Jesus is saying and suggest that Jesus has fallen into a pessimistic frame of mind from which he needs rescue. Peter does not realize, of course, that such a death lies at the heart of the Messiah's mission and at the centre of a new and victorious kingdom. As Jesus says, Peter has fallen victim to human thinking: "You do not have in mind the concerns of God, *but merely human concerns*" (8:33b). In other words, human notions of kingship involving either military triumph or earthly glory are as far removed from Jesus's thinking as the prospect of humiliation and death being the path to glory and victory is from Peter's. Jesus sees the cross followed by resurrection as the essential way of building a new kingdom, whereas for Peter, a violent death seems like abject failure. Jesus considers Peter's attitude a sell-out to Satan (8:33). And Peter considers Jesus unnecessarily pessimistic.

How did Jesus come to know and understand his destiny as a sacrifice for sin? For Jesus, as the Son of Man (a phrase drawn from the apocalyptic title for the glorious Messiah in Daniel 7:13), such knowledge or understanding probably came in several ways. It must have come from his communion with the Father, by the operation of the Spirit who filled him at his baptism (Mark 1:10), and from his study of the Scriptures, notably Daniel and Isaiah (especially chapters 40–66). The image of the Suffering Servant in Isaiah must have been especially formative (see Isaiah 52:13–53:12, particularly) together with the picture of the Son of Man in Daniel 7 and in the psalms, such as in Psalm 22. Jesus knew he was called to be a sacrifice for human sin.

The Cross, or his crucifixion, lay at the heart of Jesus's mission. In preceding months in the region of Galilee and based in Capernaum, Jesus revealed the nature of the kingdom he was initiating, and which, because of his presence, was "near" (Mark 1:15), through the trouncing of disease, the overcoming of death, the subordination of the Devil, and authority over creation. *Yet people could enter this kingdom or come under this rule only through the way of the Cross.* They must receive forgiveness and redemption through faith in the work of the Cross. As Peter said later in his first epistle, "'He himself bore our sins' in his body on the cross, so that we might die to sins and live for righteousness" (1 Peter 2:24). Peter had by then come to understand what at first sight seemed like defeatist talk but was in fact the path to victory. In a piece of writing from the Early Church called the Epistle to Diognetus (c. AD 150), the unknown author writes about the Cross in these terms:

> But when the time arrived that God planned to reveal at last his
> goodness and power (Oh the supreme beneficence and love of
> God!), he did not hate us, destroy us, or hold a grudge against us.
> But he was patient, and bore with us, and out of pity for us he took

our sins upon himself. He gave up his own Son as a ransom for us: the holy one for the lawless, the innocent one for the wicked, the righteous for the unrighteous, the imperishable one for the perishable, the immortal one for the mortal. For what else could hide our sins but the righteousness of that one? How could we who were lawless and impious be made upright except by the Son of God? O the sweet exchange! Oh, the inexpressible creation! Oh, the unexpected acts of beneficence! That the lawless deeds of many should be hidden by the one who was upright, and the righteousness of one should make upright the many who were lawless.[7]

The Cross was then the God-ordained means of forgiveness and reconciliation, whereby alienated humankind could be reconciled to a holy and loving God. Jesus took the shame, the punishment and the guilt, so that through faith in him others might go free—acquitted, justified and freed. Yet the Cross was not only a once-for-all event procuring freedom, it was also to be a symbol of a way of life.

The Cross as a way of life

Jesus immediately goes on to speak of the Cross as a way of life. "Whoever wants to be my disciple must deny themselves, take up their cross and follow me" (Mark 8:34). What he is saying is that the Cross is not just a single event, but also a way of living. If abandonment is at the heart of Jesus's sacrifice, it is also to be the essence of our Christian way of life. It is open palm living. It is giving rather than holding onto. It is abandoning life rather than preserving it. This style of living is summed up by Jesus saying, "Whoever wants to save their life will lose it, but whoever loses their life for me and for the gospel will save it" (8:35).

There is a prayer written by Archbishop Thomas Cranmer for the season of Lent that encapsulates this so well:

Almighty God, whose most dear Son, went not up to joy but first he suffered pain, and entered not into glory before he was

crucified: mercifully grant that we, walking in the way of the
cross, may find it none other than the way of life and peace:
through Jesus Christ our Lord.

To walk the way of the Cross is risky living. I have recently returned
from Egypt, a visit made at the invitation of the Coptic Church. In recent
years, the Christians in Egypt have suffered much from terrorist attacks,
with many made martyrs for their faith. While attending a church there
in Heliopolis, called St Mark's, I saw a security fence around the church,
two policemen sitting outside with guns and an airport-style security
gate through which worshippers must pass. Inside, I noticed that the
priest taking the liturgy always held a Coptic cross in his hand, and with
it blessed both adults and children. It was as if they were all saying, we
are committed to the values of the Cross and to abandoning our future
into the hands of the God of the Cross. In the end it will always be a way
of life and, at the deepest level, a way of peace. Thus, says Jesus, don't be
ashamed of *this way* or of me, for you will discover after the crucifixion
and resurrection that through these things "the kingdom of God has
come with power" (8:38–9:1).

The Transfiguration

On reflection, it should come as no surprise that the Transfiguration
happened so soon, just six days after the formal confession of Jesus as
the Messiah (the Anointed One or Christ). It must have had a double
purpose: reassurance for Jesus as he faced the road to Jerusalem, his
passion and crucifixion; and an unmistakeable and powerful witness to
the chosen three disciples that Jesus, fully understood, was the fulfilment
of all the expectations of the Old Testament.

The Transfiguration either took place on a spur of Mount Hermon
near to Caesarea Philippi, or on one of the three mountains reaching over
four thousand feet to the south-east of Caesarea Philippi, or perhaps on
Mount Tabor, nearer to Galilee. The eyewitness details of the account
strengthen the historicity of the occasion: Peter unusually calls Jesus
"Rabbi"; there is a curious conversation in which Peter, overwhelmed,

promises to put up three shelters for the participants of this summit conference; and Jesus's glory is symbolized in a shining face and brilliant, radiant clothing (Mark 9:3).

The status and authority of Jesus are enhanced, especially among a Jewish audience, by the appearance of Moses and Elijah, who represent the Law and the Prophets, the two great divisions of God's Revelation to Israel. Often people ask how Moses and Elijah were recognized. It was probably as much spiritual intuition as any specific clues (I don't suppose Moses carried tablets of stone or that Elijah arrived by chariot, but something about their demeanour must have made them recognizable!). Their presence not only further reveals Jesus's status, but they are there because Jesus is also the fulfilment of their work. Jesus is the end of the law (Romans 10:4) that is represented by Moses, and he fulfils all that prophets have spoken (Luke 24:25). Thus, the presence of Moses and Elijah underlines the fulfilment that Jesus brings to the law's demands and to the prophecies of the Old Testament. In both respects Jesus fulfils all these Old Testament expectations. Critically, we are told by Luke that the topic of their conversation is Jesus's departure (Luke 9:31) or, quite literally, his Exodus, that is his death. It is not known exactly what they say, but presumably there is a recognition of the significance of the Cross. For Jesus it is surely strengthening to know that he is fulfilling the divine plan, laid out over centuries by the law and the prophets.

Furthermore, as they talk, further affirmation of Jesus's identity and status is given. A cloud overshadows them—a familiar picture of divine glory in the Old Testament (see Exodus 16:10; 20:21; 24:15 and 2 Chronicles 5:13) as well as of the mystery of Godhead. And from this cloud that denotes the presence of God a voice speaks, as at Jesus's baptism, and with the same words: "This is my Son, whom I love. Listen to him" (Mark 9:7). This declaration has three parts: an affirmation of Jesus's identity as the Son of God; an affirmation of the Father's love for him; and a command to listen to him. No declaration could be more complete or consequently more demanding, for listening has the meaning of obedience. For the disciples it is a command to take into the future; for Jesus it is deeply reassuring to hear the Father's affirmation of love as he contemplates the Cross.

And then, as suddenly and unexpectedly as it began, it is over and everything returns to a new normal. In keeping with the so-called Messianic secret present in the Gospel, Jesus tells Peter, James and John to remain silent about what they have seen, at least until "the Son of Man [has] risen from the dead" (9:9). For their part the disciples query, as well they might, what rising from the dead actually means. And they quiz Jesus about the Jewish expectation that Elijah (whom they have just seen) will come to prepare the way for the Messiah (see Malachi 4:5). As far as Jesus is concerned, Elijah has already come in the person of John the Baptist (Matthew 11:7–15; 17:11–13). Then, fresh from their mountaintop experience, Jesus and the disciples have to confront the reality of a spiritual struggle in a young boy.

On coming down the mountain they find quite a scene (Mark 9:14–15). A large crowd of people is gathered: a group of scribes, probably arguing with Jesus's disciples, a distraught father, and a perplexed and distressed boy—each with their own issues. The scribes doubtless seeking to make theological points, the father desperate for his son's healing, the son bemused and suffering, and the disciples frustrated and perhaps almost angry at their spiritual impotence. In the midst of all this, and fresh from the Transfiguration, Jesus arrives with the three disciples, no doubt still somewhat overwhelmed by what they have just experienced. Each will come to Jesus with their questions and doubts. Jesus's opening gambit, given the volume and excitement of the debate, is, "What are you arguing with them (the disciples) about?" (9:16). He hears from the father the nature of the son's problems, afflicted as he is by an evil spirit that frequently threatens his life in awful ways and prevents speech. Jesus is frustrated by the general lack of faith: the scribes with their theologizing, the disciples with their inability to help, and the father, whose anxiety for his son clouds his hopes of a cure by Jesus. To this father Jesus majestically says, "All things are possible to him who believes" (9:23) and promptly heals the boy by delivering him of the evil spirit.

When the disciples later ask privately why they have failed to heal the boy, Jesus says, "This kind can come out only by prayer" (9:29, some texts add "and fasting"). Perhaps the disciples have approached this deliverance too blithely. Perhaps they assume on the basis of previous experience (see 6:13) that it will all happen as it did before. Perhaps they need to remember the principle that "apart from me you can do nothing" (John 15:5). At any rate it is a lesson they will be unlikely to forget.

As he leaves the place of this incident, no doubt with that conversation with Moses and Elijah still in his mind, Jesus seeks to tell the disciples about the future in private. But they neither understand nor in their confusion ask Jesus to clarify what he means (Mark 9:32), as they are afraid to do so. Afraid, that is, of seeming dull, or afraid of the reality of which Jesus speaks, or afraid of the truth he is sharing, because the time in Galilee has been so wonderful.

We can imagine Peter explaining all this to Mark in Rome before Mark wrote his Gospel. "It was the turning point," Peter might have said, "a crossroads. In a flash of inspiration, I identified him as the Messiah, but I was blind to the future. His mind was now set on the path to the cross. That was his destiny, as Moses and Elijah somehow knew. From then on, he was the King who *must* die. In the end, I understood it and wrote of it in my letter to the churches in Asia: 'He himself bore our sins' in his body on the cross, so that we might die to sins and live for righteousness; 'by his wounds you have been healed'" (1 Peter 2:24). "Furthermore," Peter might have added, "my confession that Jesus was the Messiah, which I made at Caesarea Philippi, was confirmed in spectacular fashion on the mountain, for 'he [Jesus] received honour and glory from God the Father when the voice came to him from the Majestic Glory, saying, "This is my Son, whom I love; with him I am well pleased." We ourselves heard this voice that came from heaven when we were with him on the sacred mountain'" (2 Peter 1:17–18).

CHAPTER 7

The Values of the Kingdom

Mark 9:33–10:45

It is not too far-fetched to imagine Mark with his parchment or Roman slate, recording verbatim the Apostle Peter's reminiscences of his life with Jesus some thirty years before, and then beginning to compose his Gospel as the Roman net starts to close in around the young church in the capital. Soon the Church will face intense persecution from Nero's capricious and cruel government, with both Peter and Paul caught up in the violent persecution of Christians, especially after the great fire of Rome in AD 64. As Tertullian, the third-century Christian writer, makes clear in his *Apologia*, Christians were the ready scapegoats for everything that went wrong in the Empire.

Anyone who lived in Rome would know well the drumbeat of the Empire. Since the death of Augustus in AD 14, the Empire had been ruled by increasingly bizarre and cruel rulers. Augustus was succeeded by Tiberius (AD 14–37). Forced to marry the wilful and high-spirited Julia, the only daughter of Augustus, and abandon his much-loved wife, Vipsania, Tiberius's persona as a successful general began to crumble. First he went into self-imposed exile in Rhodes, then he made a pleasure palace in Capri—the remains of which are still visible today—where he indulged himself with slave boys and prostitutes. His rule was succeeded by those of Claudius, Caligula and Nero. The last two manifest increasing signs of instability and cruelty. Nero ruled from AD 54–68, surely at a time when Mark was in Rome with Peter. Infamous for killing both his mother and his wife Poppaea, Nero descended into ever greater viciousness, throwing off the restraint of his former tutor Seneca. And why is all this important? This is the Roman background to the use and abuse of power. If the imperial family was riddled with ambition, corruption and malice, Rome itself was founded on the pursuit of glory, military victory and subjugation. It was for this love of praise and glory that Augustine, in the *City of God*, criticized Rome.[8] Indeed, in his work *De Republica*, Cicero himself acknowledges that it "was greed for glory" that inspired his Roman ancestors. But now, in these next two chapters, we see the emergence of a kingdom with very different values, and at its head a very different king.

"What were you arguing about on the way?"

There was plenty of time to talk while walking. The disciples walked with Jesus from the slopes of Mount Hermon, past the Golan Heights to Mount Tabor, and then on to Capernaum on the Sea of Galilee or Tiberias Having no doubt overheard some of their rather overheated conversation, Jesus asks them, "What were you arguing (literally 'dialoguing') about on the road?" (Mark 9:33). Even as Jesus asks the question, they become sheepish and silent. He knows very well the theme of their argument: which of them is the greatest, or who is greater than the rest?

Like so many others, both then and now, they were into the business of comparing themselves and grading the results. It was the way the Roman Empire was ordered on what was called the *Cursus Honorum*, a ladder of offices by which an ambitious Roman might climb in seniority and power until he reached the top. The disciples had no way of getting onto such a ladder, in fact, reserved as it was for the most part for those of senatorial rank, but the idea of superiority and of comparing themselves with others, and ranking people accordingly, was nevertheless still deeply ingrained in the wider culture. Presumably in Jewish society, those in the Sanhedrin, or those who were rabbis, scribes or Pharisees, were accorded greater honour. It is an insidious thing and is fostered in contemporary areas of life through social media. It feeds on appearance, wealth, qualifications, friendships and wealth. These are the modern criteria for deciding who is the greatest. It is said that the average millennial clicks on the internet 157 times a day.[9]

Jesus gives his squabbling disciples a memorable piece of teaching about the values of his kingdom. First he turns the normal measures of importance or significance on their heads. The one who is served is usually regarded as more important than the one who serves. Not so in his kingdom. The first in importance is the servant of all. Humble service is considered of greater value than the exertion of power or the attainment of position. The last is first and the first is last. To reinforce this, Jesus wraps his arms around a small child, and says anyone who welcomes or serves this child, "welcomes both me and my Father who sent me" (9:36–37). It is a visual illustration I imagine his disciples did not quickly forget.

Recently I watched a television documentary about Princess Alice, the mother of Prince Philip. A great-granddaughter of Queen Victoria, born in Buckingham Palace, raised in Hesse, and married to the King of Greece until his forced abdication, she found herself in Athens during the Nazi occupation. At great risk to herself, she established soup kitchens there, helped Jewish families escape, and joined an order of nuns. In this, she resembled her beloved aunt, Grand Duchess Elisabeth, who after the murder of her husband by the Bolsheviks gave herself to helping the poor and founded the Order of the Holy Martyr Elisabeth. Although born "first" she was among her people as one who served.

A generous orthodoxy

In his more intemperate days, when he is ready to call down fire on unbelieving Samaritan villagers (Luke 9:54) and is nicknamed, along with his brother, a "Son of Thunder" by Jesus, the Apostle John asks Jesus on this journey to Jerusalem how to treat a group who are driving out demons in Jesus's name, but who are "not one of us". It is an invidious phrase: "not one of us". It is used by politicians, leaders and ethnic groups to identify, draw attention to and exclude others as different and hence unworthy of inclusion. John seems to be taking the view that if they are not with us, they must be against us. Jesus takes the opposite view, however: if someone is not against us, then they are with us. In that sense, his is a generous orthodoxy. In other words, those who march in a different group, but still recognize Jesus's authority by casting out demons in his name (Mark 9:38), are to be welcomed, included and given co-operation. In a church that has so many working parts, marching under so many slightly different banners and doctrines, our default position needs to be one of co-operation rather than suspicion, withdrawal and exclusion. There may be occasions when co-operation is impossible because a cardinal teaching is denied or a moral position is untenable, but the starting point is "whoever is not against us is for us" (9:40).

In 1908, the writer and poet G. K. Chesterton, an Anglo-Catholic and later a Roman Catholic, published his book *Orthodoxy*. It quickly became a classic *apologia* (defence) of Orthodox Christianity at a time when it was fashionable to downplay the miraculous and deny many of the miracles in both Old and New Testaments. In an amusing aside on the trend to disbelieve—even in his day before the First World War—Chesterton wrote, "It is common to find trouble in the parish because a parish priest cannot admit that St Peter walked on water, yet how rarely do we find trouble in a parish because the clergyman says that his father walked on the Serpentine."[10] For Chesterton, one of the defining characteristics of Jesus was his joy: "There was one thing that was too great for God to show us when he walked upon our earth: and I have sometimes fancied it was his mirth."[11] Perhaps a reason for his joy was his willingness to see the possibilities in others.

Self-discipline (Mark 9:42–50)

There is an extraordinary range to Jesus's teaching about the values of his kingdom, with verses that take us from subversive principles to revolutionary single-mindedness. At the outset of this section, we see the topsy-turvy nature of the kingdom: the least is the greatest, and the greatest the least. Such a reversal of accepted worldly values is further demonstrated by incidents and teachings throughout the Gospels: the widow whose two copper coins are worth more than the gifts of all the wealthy (Luke 21:3); the Samaritan who is the despised hero of the parable that bears his name (Luke 10:25–37); the child who is the model of how to receive the kingdom of God (Mark 10:15); and the dying thief who is taken into paradise, saying with his last breath: "Remember me when you come into your kingdom" (Luke 23:42). The Gospels are full of such subversive actions that undermine accepted norms and are praised by Jesus. Yet if we were to think that such seeming abandonment of convention means we can avoid great personal responsibility, we would be gravely mistaken.

These verses are some of the most severe in the Gospels. They are warnings expressed in all the vivid and shocking language of a prophet. It is the picture language of a Hebrew poet. The warnings are to those who lead astray "little ones", referring not so much to children as to the dependent and vulnerable members of the community. Such people can be robbed of their money, manipulated by a power-crazed leader, or stripped of their dignity. For those who do that, "it would be better for them if a large millstone were hung round their neck and they were thrown into the sea" (Mark 9:42). Others are told to avoid falling into sinful ways at all costs. Better to cut off the offending limb metaphorically than lead such a one astray. The message is to have nothing to do with the fruitless ways of darkness (Ephesians 5:11), and to this end exercise self-discipline, which is one of the fruits of the Spirit (Galatians 5:22–23).

Remaining loyal (Mark 10:1–12)

One of the topics that came up regularly between the Pharisees and Jesus was divorce. This was in part because there were two schools of Rabbinic thought on the subject: Rabbi Shammai held that divorce was only permissible for the most serious offence, whereas Rabbi Hillel permitted divorce for the most trivial things, like burning a meal.

The Pharisees now approach Jesus with this pastoral chestnut to see where he stands in the debate. For Jesus, the issue is not the comparatively frivolous debate between these two rabbis but has a much more profound meaning for him.

Jesus asks what Moses commanded, and here the Pharisees would have called to mind the injunction in Deuteronomy 24:1–4, where Moses says a husband may divorce his wife if "he finds something indecent about her", but having divorced her, cannot re-marry her if, in the meanwhile, she has married another who has died. Jesus says these arrangements are hardly a gold standard for marriage, and they have a seemingly provisional nature. His view about this certificate of divorce is that it is not ideal and is only permitted because of "hardness of heart" (Mark 10:5). The original intention for marriage persists for all time and is that "a man will leave his father and mother and be united to his wife, and the two will become one flesh . . . Therefore, what God has joined together, let no one separate". We cannot help but notice that this ordinance is for male and female (10:6–9).

There is no promise more sweeping and comprehensive than that which bride and groom say to each other on their wedding day. In the Anglican wedding service, the words, hallowed by the ages, are breathtaking, risky, awesome and profligate: "With my body I honour you, all that I am I give to you and all that I have I share with you within the love of God, Father, Son and Holy Spirit." Marriage is a "union to end all unions, the very last word, and the first, in human intimacy. Socially, legally, physically, emotionally, every which way, there is just no other means of getting closer to a human being, and never has or will be, than in marriage."[12] But it needs to be sustained over twenty, fifty and even sixty years by love, intimacy, the gift of children or extended family, friendships, prayer, conversation, silence, wonder, forgiveness and more forgiveness, shared goals, shared joys and griefs, and partnership.

Of course, not every marriage succeeds. But in a sequel to the initial conversation, only now with only the disciples (10:10–12), Jesus spells out the gravity of divorce. It is not that adultery is the unforgivable sin, but divorce leaves deep wounds. And in a world where divorce had become too easily obtained by many men, it was a shock to discover that Jesus was calling them to work at their marriages rather than discard their wives like old shoes. Could it be that Jesus's teaching about marriage, quite apart from being true in itself, protects the more vulnerable party from exploitation?[13]

If, in his teaching about marriage, Jesus implicitly raises the dignity of women, he does the same for children. He rebukes his disciples for preventing people bringing their children to him for his blessing (10:13). Taking the children in his arms, he blesses them and praises their qualities.

They are examples of how to receive the kingdom of God. They are full of open-hearted trust.

The eye of a needle (Mark 10:17–31)

In many ways, the clue to this hard-hitting conversation between Jesus and the Rich Young Ruler is in the young man's opening question, and quite possibly his demeanour, which is at once attractive and flawed. After all, we are told that Jesus "loves him" (Mark 10:21). Yes, Jesus loves all people, but for Mark, once again recording Peter's memory of this meeting, there must have been something special about Jesus's conversation with and reaction to this young man. What might Jesus have loved *in* him? His eagerness—falling on his knees before him? His spiritual quest for eternal life (10:17)? Or simply that indefinable quality of human personality that can make someone appealing? Perhaps it was any or none of these things. Yet what Jesus must have seen was a well-educated, rich, possibly charming individual who was on a serious spiritual quest, else he would not have come, he would not have knelt, and he would not have made himself vulnerable. And now to his question, *what must I do* to inherit eternal life?! Perhaps the answer that is coming is what you should do, you cannot do on your own, and what you can do is not enough.

So, let's begin with what he thinks he can do. Jesus forewarns him that this will not be an easy conversation, saying, "Why do you call me good?", begging a question as to his identity, for only God is truly good (10:18). Jesus then himself enumerates the second part of the decalogue (the Ten Commandments) and asks if the young man has kept them. He replies that he has, and may have, in so far as he has not broken them *in deed*. But we know that Jesus extends their remit to cover not just deeds, but thoughts also (Matthew 5:17ff.), which would make none of us as confident of compliance as the young man is.

Seeing that the young ruler is still so confident in himself, Jesus shows him the boundary of his ability. By challenging him to sell everything and give to the poor, he shows something he cannot do without help. It is not that "selling all" is a requirement for becoming a disciple, as we know from elsewhere (see Acts 2:37–38), but in challenging this man,

Jesus shows him that without grace, without that encounter and epiphany in his soul, *he* would find it beyond him. Of course, some have divested themselves of great wealth: Basil of Caesarea, Francis of Assisi, Ignatius of Loyola, or the twentieth-century missionary C. T. Studd, and many others, no doubt, but not the Rich Young Ruler, at least not that day.

Jesus then uses this moment to teach about the power of money or possessions. They can easily gain a controlling influence in a person's life. Wealth of itself is not wrong: it is how you obtain it and what you do with it. It can be a snare and can make entering the kingdom as hard as a camel going through the eye of a needle. How is it that money can exercise such control? Acquiring it can become an overriding ambition, retaining it an anxious preoccupation, and possessing it can be a spiritual stronghold. Generosity is the best way of keeping its influence in check. God loves a hilarious giver! (2 Corinthians 9:7b).

Hearing all this, the disciples, and Peter in particular, become concerned. For a start, what may seem impossible with human beings, giving away wealth, is in fact quite possible through God's power (Mark 10:27). Furthermore, sacrifices and generosity in the service of the kingdom are noted and will be rewarded in this age, even with persecutions, and in the age to come with eternal life.

The best seats

It seems that the disciples were at times riven with rivalry, competitiveness and ambition. And given that, not so long before, Jesus has praised the example of children who receive the kingdom of God with simplicity and faith (Mark 10:15) and has rebuked his disciples for arguing about who is the greatest (9:33–35), it seems rather obtuse of James and John to seek the best seats in the coming kingdom (10:37). Their obtuseness is to our benefit, however, as once again it elicits from Jesus teaching that is of remarkable power and importance.

James and John are one of two sets of brothers among the disciples. More than that, they are part of the inner circle of three, and are thus accorded remarkable privileges by Jesus. Most recently they have witnessed the Transfiguration (9:2–13). But this treatment has gone to their heads and now they come to Jesus and ask with amazing brashness that he do for them whatever they ask (10:35). This request is breathtaking in its assumptions and in its misplaced sense of entitlement. Then Jesus graciously draws them out about *what* they have in mind, and they answer that they want the *best seats* in his forthcoming kingdom, meaning places of authority and power on his right and left side.

If Jesus is taken aback by their naked ambition, he doesn't say so. What he does highlight is that they do not know what they are asking (10:38). As yet they don't know very much about his kingdom, and especially how it will be fully inaugurated by his death and resurrection. They don't know that its inception is to be bathed in suffering and blood. Jesus challenges them by asking whether they can "drink the cup" (10:38) that he must drink, referring to the cup of suffering about which he prays in the Garden of Gethsemane (14:36), or be baptized with the baptism he must undergo. Not only must Jesus drink this cup, but he must be baptized or immersed in its suffering.

In other words, privileges in the kingdom will go especially to those who suffer for them (see Revelation 7:9ff.). When asked if they can do this, James and John in unison blithely say "we can" (10:39). They do not lack self-confidence! And in truth James will be martyred and beheaded (Acts 12:2). And John, although spared a violent death (see John 21:20–23), may well have suffered as an exile in a hard labour camp on the island of Patmos (Revelation 1:9). Jesus leaves their confidence about drinking the cup and enduring the baptism of which he speaks and closes the conversation by simply saying such privileges in the kingdom are not his to give but are already allocated! (10:40). But there is then a final and all-important epilogue to this conversation.

The rest of the disciples are understandably incensed that James and John have approached Jesus with their request. They need not have worried, but such is their desire for preferment they too resent the brothers' jockeying for position. It is another opportunity for Jesus to explain the nature of the kingdom he is establishing and the style of his kingship. He draws a fundamental distinction between his own rule and that of the Gentile rulers, not least their own rulers in Palestine and in Rome. They "lord it over" (10:42) their subjects, which is never the way of Christian leadership (see 1 Peter 5:1–4, especially verse 3, which shows that Peter has clearly learnt this lesson). This is not to be the way of leading. Once again, the kingdom of God turns normal expectations about the exercise of authority upside down: "Whoever wants to become great among you must be your servant, and whoever wants to be first must be slave of all" (10:43–44) (The word *doulos*, meaning slave, is used here and not the Greek word for servant, *diakonos*, found earlier in 9:35). With these words Jesus inaugurates the pattern of the servant king.

Finally, and by way of rounding off this conversation, Jesus delivers his *coup de grace*, which is the perfect French idiom for what he now says. "The Son of Man," he says, "did not come to be served, but to serve, and to give his life as a ransom for many" (10:45). This is one of the most important verses in the entire Gospel. Not only does it give us a model for all leadership for all time, but it also explains that Jesus's sacrificial death is the means of ransoming the human race from darkness, death and the dominion of Satan (see Colossians 1:13). The Cross, and the redemptive sufferings of Jesus, are to be the entry point to the kingdom. Faith in what Jesus has achieved on the cross is to be the turnstile at the entrance. As Athanasius puts it in his famous work *De Incarnatione*: "The lord stretched out his hands, that with the one he might draw the ancient people and with the other those from the Gentiles, and join both together in himself."[14]

This whole section highlights the values of the new kingdom Jesus has come to establish and proclaim. In this kingdom, there will be a reversal of accepted human norms: "Many who are first will be last, and the last first" (Mark 10:31). In this kingdom, there will be a generous orthodoxy in which we should assume that those who are not against us are for us (9:39). It is a kingdom in which the highest standards of integrity and self-discipline pertain (9:47), and in which enduring loyalty to our spouses fulfils the intention of marriage (10:7–9). It is a kingdom where the natural simplicity and faith of a child is an example to all its citizens (10:15). It is a kingdom where grace may prise what is commonly most precious to us, namely money, from our hands (10:22). And lastly, it is a kingdom where service rather than personal glory is our aim, following a king who gives his life as a ransom for all (10:45).

As Jesus says to his disciples for a third time (10:32–34), he must go to Jerusalem, where "the Son of Man will be delivered over to the chief priests and teachers of the law. They will condemn him to death and will hand him over to the Gentiles, who will mock him and spit on him, flog him and kill him. Three days later he will rise" (10:33, 34). Despite knowing this, "Jesus [leads] the way and the disciples [are] astonished" (10:32). Little do they understand what awaits Jesus and themselves in the days ahead. Mark will use six chapters, a third of his Gospel, describing these days.

CHAPTER 8

The Wisdom of the King

Mark 10:46–12:44

While Mark was staying in Rome (1 Peter 5:13), he surely would have heard about the Triumphs of the Roman Emperors, even from the very architecture of Rome itself. For some years there had not been a Triumph such as when Rome celebrated the conquest of Britain in the reign of Claudius in AD 43. In the heyday of Augustus's reign, there had been several Triumphs, none more spectacular than the three-day celebrations of his victories in Illyria, Actium and Egypt in 29 BC.[15] For his part, Nero would hold a kind of Triumph when the Armenian King Tiridates came to do obeisance before him as a client king on the eastern edge of the Empire in AD 66. In a full Triumph, when the Emperor passed in his chariot through the adoring crowd, on whom he frequently lavished "bread and circuses", a slave was reputed to ride alongside the Emperor and whisper in his ear "you are only a mortal".

When Jesus embarked on his triumphant entry into Jerusalem, he had not a chariot, but a donkey. There was no need for a slave to whisper in his ear since he was more than a mortal. He was *dei filius*, and his triumph was to end with a seemingly ignominious death followed by a victorious resurrection, not in days of feasting and gladiatorial combat and games. For Mark, composing his Gospel in Rome, there could not have been a greater contrast: a Roman Emperor luxuriating in the praise of his citizens, partly as a result of bribes, and Jesus, whose triumphant arrival in Jerusalem was remarkably simple, and who was inaugurating another kingdom, as the crowd recognized (Mark 11:10).

The style of Jesus's entry into Jerusalem is prefigured in a passage that involves passing through Jericho. As he leaves Jericho, Jesus is addressed royally as the Son of David and is then asked to restore the sight of a blind beggar, Bartimaeus. Jesus grants the man's insistent request for mercy and, now seeing, Bartimaeus joins the procession following Jesus to Jerusalem (10:46–52). The event is an indication of the mercy that lies at the heart of this journey to Jerusalem.

Jesus's triumphant entry into Jerusalem

The approach to Jerusalem is always dramatic, and nowhere more so than when approached by the Mount of Olives. Rising to almost three thousand feet, the Mount of Olives faces the Temple Mount, with the powerful outline of a temple newly renovated by Herod the Great and his successors. Jesus will soon be teaching in the Temple Courts. As he breasts the brow of the hill, with Jerusalem coming into view, Jesus pauses, Luke tells us, and then weeps over the city, saying "If you, even you, had only known on this day what would bring you peace—but now it is hidden from your eyes" (Luke 19:41–42). At some point before entering the city or beginning his descent, Jesus sends two of his disciples to collect a young colt upon which he will ride into Jerusalem, fulfilling the prophet Zechariah's prediction that the Messiah will ride humbly, but majestically, into Jerusalem "on a colt, the foal of a donkey" (Zechariah 9:9; Mark 11:2). The colt is provided by an unknown owner with whom either a pre-arranged plan has been made to lend it, or with whom the name of Jesus, the Lord, is sufficient to procure it, with the promise of a safe return (11:3).

A crowd gathers spontaneously and offers praise: some spread cloaks in the path of the donkey; others cut down branches of palm trees and slew them in Jesus's path, in imitation of the greeting of a king (2 Kings 9:12–13). Different members of the crowd, including children, cry out acclamations of praise including "Hosanna", which means "save now" in Aramaic and which is taken from Psalm 118:25 and used in celebrations during the Feast of Tabernacles.[16] Other shouts of praise mingle with "Hosanna", such as "Blessed is he who comes in the name of the Lord" (Psalm 118:25–26) and, perhaps more revealingly, "Blessed is the coming kingdom of our father David" (Mark 11:9–10).

THE WISDOM OF THE KING

For all who recognize this event of Jesus riding into Jerusalem as a kingly moment of the Messiah entering the capital of Israel, it is in reality a veiled assertion of his kingly power. Yes, Jesus chooses to fulfil the prophetic prediction of Zechariah, and later the disciples will look back on the event with fresh understanding (John 12:16). Yet at the time it is a comparatively low-key moment. Mark speaks of "many" (Mark 11:8) being there, rather than huge crowds. Although Matthew says that "the whole city was stirred" with anticipation (Matthew 21:10), Jesus's kingship is for the discerning. The procession has a very quiet ending. Jesus looks around the Temple Courts then leaves the city and retires to Bethany, his base. It is the beginning of the last week of his earthly life. His triumphant entry has been typically understated and veiled, but over the week it is clear that the kingdom he has come to usher in is on a path of confrontation, both with the Jewish leaders and with Roman power.

Judgement now and later (Mark 11:12–12:12)

The next few sections, the Cursing of the Fig Tree, the Cleansing of the Temple and the Parable of the Tenants, are all about the judgement of Israel, with a push back by its leaders about the authority of Jesus (Mark 11:22–33). The role of Israel in God's salvation plan is part of what Paul calls the mystery hidden in the ages (Ephesians 3:2–6). In broadest terms, God's plan is to rescue a people composed of Israelites and Gentiles who *together* will become stewards of a renewed creation (see Ephesians 1:9, 10), a new people with a new mandate and task. But the deep paradox is that for this to be achieved, the Son of Man must be rejected, crucified in a great act of atonement and raised from the dead, the first fruits of a new created order. The rejection of Israel's Messiah by that nation's own leaders becomes the focus of Jesus's action and teaching in this section. Yet the rejection by Israel of its Messiah is the occasion for this new deal (covenant) between God and the entire created order, including humanity (see Acts 2:22, 23, 29–34).

What we see here in these verses is the judgement of Israel, not its abandonment (Paul goes into this in much greater length in Romans 9 and 10). And the first act of judgement is the cursing of the fig tree. At first glance, and even second glance, this miracle is extremely difficult. After all, it is the only destructive miracle in the corpus of miracles throughout the Gospels. It is not about Jesus cursing a fig tree in a fit of pique because it has no fruit on it when out of season, and because he is hungry. The fig tree is a symbol of Israel, and this fig tree is like Israel, all leaves and no residual fruit or, as Isaiah puts it, "These people come near to me with their mouth and honour me with their lips, but their hearts are far from me" (Isaiah 29:13). For this the tree is judged or cursed and shrivels up. A spirituality of all words and no heart will in the end prove fruitless. Although not yet understanding the significance of what is done, Peter understands the sub-plot, namely Jesus's power, and Jesus uses Peter's observation to teach about the power of faith, especially when it is uncluttered by unforgiveness (Mark 11:25).

A further example of the judgement of Israel is the Cleansing of the Temple (11:15–19). Jesus must have walked through the Temple precincts on many occasions, but this is the moment he decides to challenge the corruption that has settled in it. In so doing he raises the temperature between himself and the religious leaders (11:18). Whereas John puts the Cleansing of the Temple at the start of his Gospel (John 2:13ff.), to demonstrate perhaps the emptiness of Temple Judaism at the outset of Jesus's ministry, Mark, Matthew and Luke place it here, its most likely chronological occurrence. The buying and selling of sacrificial animals and suchlike with the Temple's own currency (hence the need for money-changers) is a blight on the purpose of the Temple, which has become a money-making machine. Although, as we shall see, Jesus knows that the days of the Temple are numbered (13:2), he sees that as no reason to take lightly the role of the Temple as a house of prayer for all nations (meaning the Gentiles). It is very probable that the buying and selling that goes on in the Court of the Gentiles gives the impression that commerce is more important than spiritual enquiry. As Jesus says, it is supposed to be a house of prayer, but the traders and temple authorities have made it a den of robbers (11:17). It is all too easy, unless we are very careful, for the custodians of great Christian buildings to go down the same path and to lose sight of their real object in the struggle to maintain them.

The third element to this judgement on Israel comes in the form of words rather than actions, and in the form of a very pointed parable—the

Parable of the Tenants. At the conclusion of the parable, the Jewish authorities who are listening, perhaps a mixture of the Sanhedrin and Pharisees, the self-appointed guardians of Judaism, realize only too clearly that Jesus is speaking about them (12:12). In many ways, the features of the parable have been laid down by the prophets of the Old Testament, not least Isaiah, who in his famous picture of Chapter 5 (5:1–7) describes God as looking for fruit in a vineyard that he himself has protected, nurtured and kept over years. Despite all the care lavished upon it, "it yielded only bad fruit" (small, hard grapes, Isaiah 5:2). As that prophecy plaintively describes, "The vineyard of the Lord Almighty is the nation of Israel, and the people of Judah are the vines he delighted in. And he looked for justice, but saw bloodshed; for righteousness, but heard cries of distress" (Isaiah 5:7).

In the parable that Jesus tells, there is increasing sadness as the lord of the vineyard repeatedly sends his messengers, the prophets, to collect the fruit, but each is beaten and sent away empty-handed. In the end, the lord sends his son, who is not beaten, but killed. For this deed punishment will be meted out, and the very "stone the builders rejected (changing the metaphor, but in so doing using the important Psalm 118:22–23) has become the cornerstone" (12:7–10).

In a single parable, Jesus encapsulates the Lord's relationship with Israel. The vineyard is his creation, from the first covenant with Abraham (Genesis 12:1–9) and its construction under Moses (Exodus 20). Yet Israel repeatedly proves faithless, ignoring the prophets and their message from the Lord. The killing of the vineyard owner's son is the moment when the vineyard will be "given to others" (12:9). In other words the Gentiles, and the future vineyard will include Jew and Gentile on the basis of belief in the Messiah, his death and resurrection. Indeed, this new community will in the New Testament succeed Israel. And the wisdom of God and the king means that Israel's rejection creates a new way of salvation and the inclusion of the Gentiles (Romans 11:25–36).

Faced with the Cleansing of the Temple, the symbolic withering of the fig tree and the Parable of the Tenants, the religious leaders push back with their own questioning of Jesus's authority, and it is no surprise that they do this, given the challenge Jesus is to their authority. A very high-powered group of Jewish leaders, including the chief priests, the teachers of the law and the elders, ask Jesus in the Temple Courts, "By what authority are you doing these things? . . . And who gave you authority to do this?" (11:28). In one sense it is a reasonable question. After all, Jesus has not come up by any recognized route: he has not been trained as a scribe or as a Pharisee, and he has not been schooled in Jerusalem or at the Temple. Yet behind the question is a desire to implicate him in a claim to be either a prophet or the Messiah, and then denigrate him. So, in the hope that he might claim to be the Messiah, they ask this question about authority.

As so often before, Jesus can see the purpose of their question, which is not genuine, but a way of trapping him. He is not prepared to give them a direct answer and, as so often, he replies with another question: "John's baptism—was it from heaven, or of human origin?" (11:30). They soon realize the cleverness and wisdom of Jesus's reply. If they say from heaven, then why didn't they believe him? If they say of human origin, they will lose the respect of the people. Aware of the pitfalls of either reply they refuse to answer, and so does Jesus. It will not be the last question aimed at catching him out; indeed there will be a veritable spate of them.

Many questions

Jerusalem was made up of several political and religious pressure groups. The ruling council or Sanhedrin was comprised of the chief priests, the lay and priestly nobility, including some Sadducees and Pharisees, who themselves belonged to different communities.[17] All of these groupings were disturbed by Jesus and his challenge to the status quo, and most wanted to break the connection between Jesus and the general population so that they might retain their own influence. To this end they wanted to discredit Jesus and so came to him with their trick questions.

First it is the turn of the Herodians—the supporters of Herod Antipas, the ruler of Galilee and the husband of Herodias, who requested the head of John the Baptist—and some Pharisees who come with a well-polished and famous question. The question, whether Jews should pay tribute money to Caesar, conceals several pitfalls. If Jesus agrees that it should be paid, it will seem as if he is complicit in the occupation of Palestine by Roman forces and their supporters. If he advocates non-payment of tribute money, then he can be framed for inciting insurrection against Rome. The Pharisees and Herodians must have been confident about tarnishing Jesus's reputation, whatever the answer. For his part, Jesus knows their hypocrisy and their intent (for they use the Roman coinage anyhow), but his divine wisdom is more than sufficient for their deceit. Famously, he asks for a denarius, the standard Roman silver coin, with the Emperor's head stamped on it. He points to the image of the Emperor, probably Tiberius, saying, "Give back to Caesar what is Caesar's and to God what is God's" (12:17). They are amazed at this wisdom.

It is not far-fetched to suppose that as he wrote, quite probably in Rome, Mark had sight of a denarius, the most common of all Rome's coins. He would have seen the image of Nero and, on the reverse, the inscription *Nero Caesar Divi Augusti Filius Augustus Pontifex Maximus*, proclaiming the Emperor a son of god. Holding it, he would have reflected on the brilliance of Jesus's answer. It does not say everything about a Christian's relationship with the state, but it underlines that beside having obligations to God, a Christian has an obligation to pay dues to the state. Later this obligation will be spelt out further (see Romans 13:1–7; 1 Timothy 2:1–6; 1 Peter 2:13–17). But here Jesus shows that he recognizes such an obligation, as well as each person's obligation to love God, which we will come to.

The next question is posed by the Sadducees, an elite religious group closely associated with the priesthood, often supplying the High Priest from among their ranks. Committed to a literal interpretation of the Law (Torah), they famously did not believe in a resurrection after death, and it this belief that lies behind their rather obscure-sounding question. In their question, they seek to pour ridicule on the idea of the resurrection by posing an extreme case. From the obligation of a Jew to marry his brother's widow and to raise up a family to his brother's name (see Deuteronomy 25:5–10), they posit the case of seven brothers who die in turn, having married their brothers' widow. In heaven, the Sadducees ask rather smugly, which one will be the husband of the woman? In response to their far-fetched question, Jesus says they are wide of the mark: "You do not know the Scriptures or the power of God" (Mark 12:24). The Scriptures uphold the idea of the resurrection, since God is called the

God of Abraham, Isaac and Jacob, and he is always the God of the living and not the dead. Furthermore, in heaven there is no marriage anyway, but humans will instead then be like the angels (12:25). The Sadducees are comprehensively corrected by Jesus, but further questions are waiting in the wings.

The next question appears to have no hidden agenda or desire to trip Jesus up. It appears genuine and straightforward, and is from one of the teachers of the law. The scribes, or teachers of the law, were another elite group in Judaism, alongside the Pharisees. Many of them were Pharisees, Sadducees or Essenes (a more monastic group of ascetic Jews from Qumran). They would have been trained in the law from an early age and were considered the guardians of true knowledge.[18] One of their number now comes to Jesus and asks him, "Of all the commandments, which is the most important?" (12:28b). In some ways, this scribe's question is a classic "chestnut". For instance, a leading rabbi, Rabbi Hillel, was asked the same, to which he replied, "What you hate for yourself, do not do for your neighbour: this is the whole Law, the rest is commentary: go and learn."[19] In his reply, Jesus puts together two commandments from the law: Deuteronomy 6:5 and Leviticus 19:18. The former is taken from the *Shema Yisrael*, which is considered the most important part of a Jew's prayers and spirituality, and the latter is almost an aside in the reiteration of various laws in Leviticus.

In bringing them together in such simplicity, Jesus provides a unique summary of all the law in two parts: our duty to God and our duty to our neighbour. And at the centre of both commandments is love: loving God and loving our neighbour. As Paul said, love is the fulfilment of the law (Romans 13:10b), or as St Augustine of Hippo daringly put it in a commentary on 1 John, "love God and do what thou wilt". Indeed, every thought or action can be judged by this standard, with the rule that everything that fulfils this standard should be followed, and all that contravenes it should be abandoned. The young scribe—for he seems youthful—is impressed and acknowledges the wisdom with which Jesus answers his question. In discerning the wisdom of Jesus's answer (Mark 12:32), he is told that he is not far from the kingdom (12:34), since he appears drawn both to the person and the teaching of the one who is manifesting that kingdom, and is at its heart.

If the teachers of the law have no further questions, Jesus asks them one instead. What follows may be part of a longer conflict-ridden conversation about the identity of the Messiah, in which Jesus maintains from Psalm 110 that the Messiah is both a descendant of David, but also David's Lord. If this is the case, as David wrote when inspired by the Spirit (12:36), then the Messiah will be both a descendant of David and greater than David. That person will be the Messiah. And this is precisely what Jewish Christians come to believe (see Romans 1:3, 4 and Mark himself, see 1:1). Jesus is saying, in an indirect way, that that which David prophesied in this psalm has come about: David's descendant is also David's Lord. For Jewish people, especially, this was a way of identifying Jesus as the Messiah, and thereby becoming Messianic Jews.

The wisdom that sees below the surface: A warning and an insight

This section concludes with a contrast. It seems it is all too easy for us humans to fall into religious pride, particularly when we think we have understood everything. It was C. S. Lewis who said that there is no fault of which we are more unconscious in ourselves than pride, and the more we have it ourselves, the more we dislike it in others.[20] The Jewish religious leaders had it in spades. They liked to be noticed, they liked conspicuous clothes, they liked deference from others, they liked important seats, they felt they deserved other people's money, even that of widows, and they liked to make a show of long prayers. In the Sermon on the Mount, Jesus contrasts the spirituality of the hypocrites with true spirituality when it comes to prayer, fasting, almsgiving and good works: the former seek human praise, the others practise their piety in secret (Matthew 6:1–18). And now, even as Jesus warns of the misleading ways of the scribes or teachers of the law, a perfect example of true generosity and humility appears.

Jesus is sitting opposite the place where people place their temple gifts. Some people come up to the "treasury" and ostentatiously deposit large amounts of money. And then a frail, elderly woman comes up and places two tiny copper coins in the treasury. Jesus calls his disciples and explains, through his insight, what she has done. He pronounces that she has put in more than all the better off: "They all gave out of their wealth; but she, out of her poverty, put in everything—all she had to live on" (12:43, 44). It is a further reminder that the Lord does not look on the outer appearance, but on the heart (1 Samuel 16:7b).

CHAPTER 9

The Labour Pains of the Kingdom

Mark 13

There is no doubt that the kingdom of God would not *fully come* until one era ended and a new one had begun. Before Mark embarks on telling us how Jesus initiated this new era with his death and resurrection (Mark 14–16), he tells us about the labour pains of this new kingdom. This teaching in Mark 13 appears to be an assembly of Jesus's teaching on the subject of the last things. It begins with a single innocent remark about the Temple itself. One disciple says, "Look, Teacher! What massive stones! What magnificent buildings!" (13:1).

The Temple was rapidly becoming one of the wonders of the world but would in fact have a tragically short shelf life. The construction so admired by one of the disciples was the Second Temple, the first having been built by Solomon (1 Kings 5, 6) and then destroyed by the Babylonians (2 Kings 25:9; 2 Chronicles 36:18, 19), after becoming a snare to Israel and even a place of idolatry (Ezekiel 10). The relatively unimpressive Second Temple was restored under Ezra in 515 BC (see Ezra 6:13ff.) but was given a complete refurbishment by Herod the Great.

Begun in 20 BC, this refurbishment programme had already lasted forty-six years. "It has taken forty-six years to build this temple, and you are going to raise it in three days?" (John 2:20). Restoration was still going on throughout Jesus's life and the work was not completed until AD 62–4. The historian Josephus wrote that some eighteen thousand people worked on the Temple and in the quarries supplying its stone. Much of the facade of the main part was covered with gold.[21] It is thus not surprising that one of the disciples remarks on the Temple to Jesus. What will have been shocking to him is Jesus's reply. Jesus says that in a matter of years, "Not one stone here will be left on another" (13:2).

In fact, the Jewish revolt against the Romans, which began in AD 66 and was at first successful in catching the Romans off guard, proved to be disastrous in the end. The culminating siege of Jerusalem by the Roman legions, led by Emperor Titus, resulted in a final stand by the Jews in the temple precincts and a devastating fire in which the temple area was destroyed (AD 70). All that was left was the platform on which the Temple had stood, with what is now known as the Wailing Wall supporting it.

After Jesus's initial statement about the fate of the Temple, there is a further conversation about its destruction while the disciples are seated on the Mount of Olives overlooking the Temple Mount. Here Jesus warns his disciples about the future.

It has been notoriously difficult to disentangle the teaching that follows, grouped together by Mark into sections that *either* refer to the time around the destruction of the Temple or refer to the times preceding the second coming of Jesus. The two events around which these warnings and teachings are grouped are the imminent destruction of the Temple and the unknown return of the Son of Man. The former is known and predicted, the date of the latter is unknown *even by the Son of Man, Jesus himself.* Jesus does not know when it will be. Although we cannot be sure which verses refer to which event, I have attempted below to connect the likely teachings to the event to which they probably refer.

About the times preceding the Temple's destruction (Mark 13:9–19)

These verses appear to refer to the forthcoming experience of the disciples in the period from c. AD 30–70. It is generally thought that Mark wrote his Gospel around AD 64, and quite possibly in Rome, where he was with Simon Peter, or shortly after he left Rome (1 Peter 5:13). If this is right, and if these verses refer to that period, then the persecution of which Jesus warns has begun and indeed has been underway for some time. Jesus tells the disciples that they must "be on [their] guard" (Mark 13:9), that they will be handed over to councils and flogged, that during this time the gospel will be preached to the nations, and that they should rely on the Holy Spirit when called before the courts (13:9–13). As we see from the early chapters of Acts, much of this swiftly takes place after the ascension: Stephen is martyred (Acts 7), likewise James, the brother of John, is executed (Acts 12:2). Peter and John are called before the Sanhedrin and threatened (Acts 4 and 12). And on several occasions Paul is flogged and imprisoned. Furthermore, the presence of the Roman legions and standards on the Temple Mount calls to mind the blasphemy committed in 168 BC by Antiochus Epiphanes, who set up a heathen altar in the Temple. Mark 13:14 refers to an "'abomination that causes desolation' standing where it does not belong" (see also Daniel 12:11). At that time especially, the bleak warnings of verses 14–19 would be very true: better not to be trapped in the city, better not to be pregnant or a nursing mother, and better not to be caught by the sudden and devastating trials of those days. The description by Josephus of those final hours of the Temple reveals it was as awful as any siege in history.[22]

The period before the Second Coming (Mark 13:5–8, 20–37)

If part of the teaching of this chapter refers to the period leading up to the destruction of the Temple and the persecution that the Church will suffer, the rest of the chapter appears to be about the period leading up to the return of Jesus, or his Second Coming. The most important point about this era is that Jesus freely admits that *he does not know* when it will be. "About that day or hour no one knows, not even the angels in heaven, nor the Son, but only the Father" (Mark 13:32).

This admission of ignorance on the part of Jesus about the date of his return has caused problems. For instance, it was a reason why, in the fourth century, those like the heretic Arius thought it meant Jesus is unlike God the Father, inferior in knowledge, and so a created being rather than one sharing the same substance as the Father. In reply, the great Coptic Bishop of Alexandria, Athanasius, when writing about these matters to another bishop called Serapion, said bluntly:

For he was made man, as it is written, and it belongs to men to be ignorant, as it belongs to them to hunger and to rest. For they [humans] do not *know* unless they hear and learn. Therefore, inasmuch as he [Jesus] was made man, he displays the ignorance which belongs to men: firstly, to show that he really has a human body, secondly, that, having in his body the ignorance of men, he might redeem his humanity from all its imperfections and cleanse it and offer it perfect and holy to the Father.[23]

For Athanasius, ignorance in this matter was proof of Jesus's humanity. But Christians, far from being able to live with ignorance themselves, have sought to put a date on Jesus's return—and, of course, those dates have mostly come and gone. Instead, what we can take from this teaching are two things: the characteristics of the age we now live in, and how to respond.

The characteristics of the age are disturbing. It is the age that spans the epoch from the ascension to the return of Jesus. Although the beauty of creation is still evident, we are aware of much dissonance, dislocation and dis-ease. Jesus talks about wars, rumours of wars, earthquakes and famines (13:7-8). We might want to add global warming, pollution of the seas and the land by plastic and waste, and destruction of habitat, biodiversity and species. And for 2020-21 we would add the global pandemic and its effects. As the Apostle Paul so powerfully wrote, the whole of creation is *groaning*, and human beings with it, for the birth of God's kingdom (Romans 8:22). Then there are those many false dawns brought about by those who claim to be Messiahs (Mark 13:6, 21, 22). Nevertheless, whenever any of the above occur, it is a cue to get ready for the return of the Messiah. And as the age proceeds, there will be increasing tension and distress (13:24, 25). All this raises the question: how then should we live?

Whenever Jesus speaks of his return, he uses one type of story and a single word to characterize the right attitude. The stories all have the dynamic of a sudden and unexpected arrival. It could be the sudden return of a master to his house, expecting to find the servants awake and waiting for him and with all in order (13:34). It could be a bridegroom coming to fetch his bride and bridesmaids for the nuptials and expecting to find them all ready. It could be a thief breaking into a house at an unexpected hour. All have the element of surprise, suddenness, unexpectedness and crisis. And the word Jesus uses most often to describe the right attitude while waiting for his return is "watch" (13:37). Watching means looking out for his return, keeping active in prayer, good works and making known his kingdom. This is the quality of discipleship most needed as we wait for his return.

In the nineteenth century, the social reformer and Christian, Lord Shaftesbury, found contemplation of the Second Coming an encouragement to his pioneering work of social reform. He was facing a difficult moment in his life in guiding legislation to reduce the working hours of child chimney sweeps, but also finding himself out on a limb politically. He wrote:

> I find myself alone, without advisers, without agents, without friends, without co-adjutators, an ancient weather-beaten rock with the seas daily receding from it. There is wisdom and mercy in all of this. It detaches one from life, and drives one more and more to pray for the Second Advent.[24]

If the disciples were called to watch for his return following Jesus's ascension, there was also a need for the same quality of spiritual alertness in the immediate events in Jerusalem around Passover. Yet the disciples will conspicuously fail to fulfil Jesus's expectations that they watch with him and pray in Gethsemane in a day's time. The disciples are about to be caught up in a rush of events, which, despite Jesus's warning, they are in no way ready to meet.

CHAPTER 10

The Costly Opening of the Kingdom

Mark 14

Mark devotes over a third of his Gospel to describing the last days of Jesus's life, ministry and crucifixion. Such an emphasis on the final days of Jesus's ministry underscores the remark made by Jesus that, "The Son of Man did not come to be served, but to serve, and to give his life as a ransom for many" (Mark 10:45). The ransom was about to be made, not with "silver or gold . . . but with the precious blood of Christ, a lamb without blemish or defect" (1 Peter 1:18–19). Mark himself was a witness to some of these events, quite possibly the arrest of Jesus in Gethsemane and his subsequent crucifixion. We will come to this. Mark's full description of the events leading up to the crucifixion becomes the template for later Gospel writers recording these events. Each Gospel writer will add unique touches from his own sources, and John was most definitely an eyewitness to these events, and in particular the crucifixion (John 19:25–27), of which he gives a vivid and telling narrative. Once Jesus arrives at the Passover Meal or Last Supper, there is an unstoppable momentum which Jesus himself has predicted (see Mark 10:33, 34) and which has been foreordained by God the Father (Acts 2:22–24). It seems like a current moving towards the most dramatic and sombre of falls. However, before Jesus himself is immersed in the cycle of trials, suffering and death by crucifixion, there is a moment of great beauty, poignancy and significance in Bethany when Jesus is anointed.

The anointing of Jesus at Bethany

There appear to be two anointings of Jesus in the Gospels: one at the house of Simon the Pharisee (Luke 7:36ff.) and another at Bethany, attended by Martha and Mary, the sisters of Lazarus whom Jesus raised from the dead and who was also there (John 12:2). According to Mark this event happens in the home of Simon the Leper in Bethany (Mark 14:1ff.), and John tells us it is Mary, the sister of Lazarus and Martha, who typically (as she was the one who loved to sit at the Lord's feet—Luke 10:39–42) pours this very expensive perfume over Jesus. It is John who gives the fullest account of what happens and has the most detail of the occasion. At any rate John's account fills out Mark's, for he tells us that it is Judas Iscariot who objects to this extravagant anointing, protesting that the costly perfume could be sold and the money given to the poor (see Mark 14:4 and John 12:4–6), although Judas is himself a thief.

The incident brings into sharp relief the issue of when to use luxury and when to give away generously, when to feast and when to fast and lament. Clearly this anointing is both a costly and sacrificial action by Mary, worthy of Jesus, but it is also a prophetic action that prepares Jesus for burial (14:8b). It reflects the earlier rhetorical question Jesus asks: "How can the guests of the bridegroom fast while he is with them?" (2:19). So there are times when extravagance is appropriate and times when it is not. This action by Mary in Bethany is one of both honouring Jesus and prophetically preparing him for the ordeal that lies ahead.

As for selling the costly perfume and giving the proceeds to the poor, as some, including Judas, are suggesting, Jesus makes a similar argument as in Mark 2, when people are querying why he and his disciples are not fasting like the Pharisees and John the Baptist (2:18–22). For Jesus, it was all a question of timing and grasping the unique moment. Quite realistically Jesus says, "The poor you will always have with you" (14:7). That is not so much a council of despair as the recognition that the opportunity for philanthropy is ongoing, while opportunities for honouring him on earth are passing. Jesus will only be on earth a few more days. This is the only time to honour and recognize him. Furthermore, this action of Mary will be an inspiration to others in their worship and service down the centuries. In fact, one could argue that it would inspire far more in others, in terms of giving and service, than the value of this particular expensive perfume.

Ironically, and tragically, it is at this point that Judas the thief, and the one who suggests cashing in the value of the perfume, now offers to betray Jesus to the chief priests for thirty pieces of silver: money that will later burn a hole in his conscience. The disciples will move back into Jerusalem with Jesus one final time. The meal is to be their last supper together and, soon after, Jesus will be arrested in Gethsemane. Events will then take their foreordained course and the fellowship of the disciples and their Lord will never be the same again.

The Last Supper

Passover was the greatest of Israel's festivals, recalling the deliverance of Israel from Egypt after the plagues and the Passover night, when the first-born Egyptians died, but the Israelites were spared (see Exodus 12; 23:14–19; Deuteronomy 16:1–8), the Angel passing over the homes daubed with the blood of a sacrificial lamb (Exodus 12:13).

The Last Supper both recalls the earlier deliverance in Egypt, and looks forward to the New Covenant, which will be made by Jesus in his blood at Golgotha. Faith in his sacrifice and in the shedding of his blood will secure forgiveness, reconciliation and acceptance.

Mark recalls that preparations for the meal are made in a somewhat cryptic fashion, rather like a meeting in a spy story: "A man carrying a jar of water will meet you. Follow him" (Mark 14:13). They appear to be having the supper on Nisan 14 in the Jewish calendar, which is in fact the day before the Passover (Nisan 15). In a large upstairs room, the customary Passover meal gets underway, but soon there are marked changes. John tells us that Jesus insists on washing his disciples' feet (John 13:2ff.). Then, as the meal proceeds, Jesus tells his disciples that one of them will betray him, which of course throws considerable suspicion and sadness over the whole meal. Although Jesus does not name Judas as his betrayer, he more or less identifies him by saying that the one who is dipping the bitter herbs into the bowl containing a sauce of dried fruits, spices and wine vinegar is the betrayer. Soon after this Judas leaves. Over time, Judas's love of money has taken control of him, and seeing the opportunity to make more he agrees to betray Jesus to the High Priest when they come to arrest him at night.

The meal continues with the first cup (the *kiddush*) being taken, the eating of the bitter herbs, the main meal, the recitation of the *haggadah* (the explanation of the Exodus story, in answer to questions from the youngest present), the first part of the Hallel (a group of psalms), followed by the second cup. At some point during the main meal Jesus takes some of the unleavened bread and, having broken it, says, "Take it; this is my body" (14:22). Likewise, over the third cup of the Passover, Jesus gives thanks for the wine, then offers it to his disciples and says, "This is my blood of the covenant, which is poured out for many" (14:24). In other Gospels, the disciples are told to do this in remembrance of him (Luke 22:19). The meal has been given a new significance: not to remember the deliverance from Egypt, but the deliverance by the Lord's death on the cross from slavery to sin and death. From now on this meal is to be a personal reminder of this liberation.

Despite the controversies down the ages as to what happens or doesn't happen to the bread or wine at the point of consecration or use, the Lord's Supper, Holy Communion or Eucharist, remains a moment of profound significance for the believer. In his great work, *Institutes of Christian Religion*, John Calvin wrote of the Eucharist, "And we ought carefully to observe, that the chief, and almost whole energy of the sacrament, consists in these words: 'It is broken for you; it is shed for you.'"[25] It is that act of eating and drinking, with faith, and remembering the Lord's death and love *for you* that is the means of grace and encourages the hope of glory. Whether taken in the home with a sick or dying person, or whether taken on pilgrimage in Jerusalem outside the Garden Tomb as I have done, whether in a small group or in a large and awesome cathedral, the significance remains the same. It is remembrance of the love of Christ demonstrated by the cross that we are ingesting with the bread and wine. So, we look back to the cross, look around at the company of the faithful, look inside to make sure we are not, like Judas, betrayers of the Lord's way, and look forward to celebrating the kingdom with the whole company of heaven and with Christ as the host (Mark 14:23). Every time we break bread and drink the cup, we celebrate the Lord's death until he comes again (1 Corinthians 11:26).

When they have finished, they sing another of the Hallel psalms, perhaps Psalm 118, which begins: "Give thanks to the Lord for he is good; his love endures for ever" (Psalm 118:1). On the way to Gethsemane, probably in light of Judas's impending betrayal and Jesus's statement that all the disciples will be scattered, Peter offers his undying loyalty. But Jesus famously responds that even that night before the cock crows, Peter will deny him three times. Yet Peter is so sure of himself, he says he would rather die than disown or deny Jesus (Mark 14:31).

Gethsemane and prayer

There are few more moving and gripping passages of Scripture than the account of Jesus's agony in the Garden of Gethsemane. This episode lies between the Last Supper and Jesus's first night-time trial at the house of the High Priest. More than anything, it demonstrates the conflict in Jesus's spirit prior to his passion and crucifixion.

The Garden of Gethsemane near Jerusalem was possibly a favourite place for Jesus. It lies just east of the Temple Mount, near to the Jericho road. Its olive trees, as old as a thousand years, still stand in the garden, close to the Church of All Nations or the Basilica of the Agony. As soon as Jesus enters the garden, he appears to be in great distress and agony. The conflict is between the divine plan of salvation, which he himself has predicted and which centres on his crucifixion, and the possibility of salvation being obtained by another way, without such suffering, both spiritual and physical. Furthermore, the conflict is between his own heightened awareness of what awaits and his disciples' seeming ignorance of impending events. The former leads Jesus to agonized prayer, while the latter sleep.

At the heart of Gethsemane is prayer. Jesus prayed much throughout his ministry: at the start of a busy day (Mark 1:35), before choosing the disciples (Luke 6:12), when he dismissed the crowd after the Feeding of the Five Thousand (Mark 6:46), and here, most of all, before his crucifixion. He seeks the support of the inner group of disciples: Peter,

James and John (14:33, 34). As he contemplates the next twenty-four hours, his soul is "overwhelmed with sorrow", and he prays on three occasions that, if possible, "the hour might pass from him" and the "cup" of suffering be taken from him (14:35, 36). But it cannot be taken away. Again, as Peter writes in his epistle, the sacrifice of the Messiah has been planned from before the foundation of the world (1 Peter 1:20). There is no turning back. Jesus, in exemplary submission and obedience, concludes his prayer, "Yet not what I will, but what you will" (14:36). And that reverent submission (see Hebrews 5:7) yields a rich harvest (Isaiah 53:10–12). Nevertheless, the prayer has prepared Jesus inwardly for the trials that lie ahead, while the sleeping of the disciples leaves them wide open to temptation. As Jesus says, "Watch and pray . . . the spirit is willing, but the flesh is weak" (14:38).

Often in prayer we do not receive what we ask for, but what we get outweighs what we think we need. As the anonymous soldier in the American Civil War wrote:

> I asked for strength that I might achieve;
> He made me weak that I might obey.
> I asked for health that I might do greater things;
> I was given grace that I might do better things.
> I asked for riches that I might be happy;
> I was given poverty that I might be wise.
> I asked for power that I might have the praise of men;
> I was given weakness that I might feel the need of God.
> I asked for all things that I might enjoy life;
> I was given life that I might enjoy all things.
> I received nothing that I asked for, all that I had hoped for.
> My prayer was answered, I was most blessed.

The arrest and trial before the High Priest

Following the nobility of Jesus's prayer, the circumstances surrounding the arrest seem contrastingly shabby, and none more so than the actions of Judas. Soon to be overcome by remorse (see Matthew 27:1–9), Judas here strides into the garden, followed by a posse of armed guards and religious leaders. Judas is surrounded by this motley crew of temple guards carrying clubs and swords, and an assortment of teachers of the law and elders of the people. They come by night so as not to attract attention, and they require Judas to identify Jesus so they can make a swift arrest. With great irony, Judas identifies and betrays Jesus with a kiss and addresses him with the respectful title "Rabbi". Yet nothing could have been more deceitful than the kiss and nothing more insincere than this address of Rabbi. We learn from John 18:10 that, in the mêlée, Peter strikes a servant of the High Priest, slicing off his ear, only for it to be immediately healed by Jesus, who on the one hand calls for a putting away of swords by his disciples, and on the other hand rebukes those who arrest him for coming after him like an insurrectionist (Mark 14:48). The truth is they are too frightened to arrest him in the open in Jerusalem. Further confusion is added by a young man slipping out of his tunic when arrested by a guard and fleeing naked out of Gethsemane (14:51–52). Tradition has it that this young man may have even been John Mark, the writer of this Gospel. What is certain is that everyone deserts Jesus (14:50), although Peter does follow at a distance (14:54). Jesus is now taken to the High Priest's house, where he is kept in a cell in the cellar before being brought for trial.

There are trials and there are trials: trials where there is a genuine exploration of the evidence before deciding guilt or innocence; and other, more political trials or show trials, where the outcome is decided before any evidence is considered by the court, such as the show trials in Stalinist Russia of the 1930s.[26] Jesus's trial is of the latter sort. The outcome is already decided, the nature of the charge is unique: that Jesus claims to be the Messiah. For most of the trial Jesus remains silent as charges are brought. These are fabricated. Mark tells us that the Jewish leaders are still looking for evidence to condemn him when the trial starts (14:55). Others have been paid to bring false evidence, but their witness statements do not agree. Still other witnesses bring to court the statement they have misunderstood—that Jesus will destroy the Temple that has been renovated over forty-five years and rebuild it in three days. In fact, he was speaking enigmatically about his own body, which will be killed and brought back to life again in three days. Jesus remains silent until the High Priest, by then exasperated, asks him point blank, "Are you the Messiah, the Son of the Blessed One?" (14:61b; see 1 Peter 2:21ff.). Jesus plainly replies, "I am" (*ego eimi*), and furthermore says that he will be seated at the right hand of the godhead and come on clouds of heaven. This is the admission that the Sanhedrin is looking for. If it is *not true* it is blasphemous, but if it is true the course of history will be changed for ever. For the High Priest, already predisposed to convict and condemn Jesus, it is more than enough. He tears his clothes. He calls for the penalty for blasphemy, which is death, to be enacted. The Sanhedrin for the most part concur. But lacking the confidence to call for immediate stoning (see John 8:59), they hand him over to the Romans for a more "judicial" death, after some initial "softening up" (Mark 14:65).

Outside in the courtyard, warming himself by the fire, sits Peter, who has followed at a distance. Maybe he has heard some of the commotion inside the High Priest's house. He is challenged by a servant girl twice and by a group of bystanders that he is one of Jesus's disciples (14:66–71). Three times he denies any connection with Jesus. In the space of minutes, he has crashed from bravado to crippling fear. He discovers the meaning of Jesus's words, "The spirit is willing, but the flesh is weak" (14:38b). Without the preparation of prayer, he is as vulnerable as a goat stalked by a leopard. Calling down curses on himself to emphasize his ignorance of Jesus, he repeats, "I don't know this man". Immediately the cock crows. He remembers Jesus's words and he breaks down and weeps (14:71, 72).

One might imagine Peter and Mark alone in a room in Rome, with Mark asking Peter to remember as much as he can of those hours, as indeed of all his time with Jesus, so that he might incorporate these memories in his Gospel. One might imagine Mark, with his stylus and parchment, recording the very words of Peter, who may himself have heard more about the trial from Nicodemus and Joseph of Arimathea, inside the High Priest's house as members of the Sanhedrin, but also as followers of Jesus. The dignity of Jesus in contrast with the shabbiness and venom of the court must have been one of their chief memories. As always, human evil lacks all nobility. As Malcom Muggeridge, the journalist and broadcaster wrote, recalling the words of the French mystic and social reformer, Simone Weil:

> What hurts most is the preference I have so often shown for what is inferior, tenth-rate, when the first rate was there for the having. Like a man who goes shopping, and comes back with cardboard shoes when he might have had leather, dried fruit when he might have had fresh, with processed cheese when he might have had cheddar, with paper flowers when primroses were out. "Nothing is so beautiful and wonderful, nothing is so continually fresh and surprising, so full of sweet and perpetual ecstasy as the good", Simone Weil writes. "No desert is as dreary, monotonous, and boring as evil".[27]

CHAPTER 11

The Crucified and Risen King

Mark 15 and 16

There is no doubt that Mark wants us to understand that at the heart of the charges against Jesus, at the centre of the soldiers mocking Jesus, and the reason for his crucifixion—as spelt out in the charge notice hammered to the cross—is that he claims to be the King of the Jews (Mark 15:26). Jesus is inaugurating a new kingdom but in a way that surpasses normal understanding. He was and is the king, the final seat of all authority.

The trial, mocking and crucifixion of the King (Mark 15:1–26)

Following the trial of Jesus in the High Priest's house and before the Sanhedrin, the decision is made by the Jewish authorities to hand Jesus over for trial by the Roman administration with the express request that he be executed (Mark 15:1). Before agreeing to the death penalty by crucifixion, Pilate wants to investigate the grounds for this charge of blasphemy and insurrection, so Jesus appears before him early in the morning (15:1).

In Mark's account, as indeed in all the synoptic Gospels, Pilate comes straight to the point, asking, "Are you the king of the Jews?" (15:2). In John's account, there is a more discursive discussion about the nature of power and truth as well as kingship (see John 18:28ff.). But Jesus, who for much of the time during this trial is silent, with, it seems, some of the Jewish leaders hurling accusations at him, replies to Pilate's question about his kingship, "You have said so." In other words, in a most low-key way, he accepts the title of king. And Mark shows that Pilate has caught on to this confession, which obviously annoys the Jews, by referring to Jesus four times as their king (15:2, 9, 12 and 26).

And yet at the heart of the Old Testament is the expectation that the great David's greater son (Jesus) will come as Messiah and King. Jesus will himself fulfil the expectations of Israel.[28] He is the king installed in Zion by the Lord (Psalm 2:6; 110). He is the king who will judge and save his people. He is the king who will usher in a new kingdom (Mark 1:15).

Mark may have seen some of the worldly trappings of kingship whilst residing in Rome: the imperial buildings, the Praetorian Guard, the deferential Senate, the vast resources at the disposal of the emperor, however unworthy. Yet in re-telling the narrative of Jesus's trial, passion and crucifixion, he sees a form of kingship that could not have been more different from all human projections. Jesus stands silently, hardly answers his accusers, accepts the description of king meekly and with a minimum of fuss, and throughout behaves majestically.

When Pilate, perceiving and sensing his innocence, has run short of ideas for liberating Jesus, he offers to release him in an act of amnesty and execute Barabbas instead (15:6–14). But the crowd brought by the Jewish leaders shouts for Jesus's crucifixion. Pilate caves in to the baying of the crowd and to the accusations of the Jews that he will be no friend of Caesar if he releases this usurper who calls himself a king. So, in a gratuitous crowd-pleasing act, Pilate frees Barabbas and has Jesus flogged, in what is an unspeakable act of torture many prisoners did not survive.

Once again it is the claim to kingship that becomes the chief narrative in the mocking of Jesus. The soldiers regard this episode as a moment of sport. They dress Jesus in a purple robe, a sign of kingship. They place a crown of thorns on his head, and a reed in his hand. And then they mock him, saying, "Hail King of the Jews", falling on their knees in fake homage (15:16–20). He is being crucified for claiming to be a king. He is too weak to carry the wooden cross, so the soldiers press Simon from Cyrene, in Libya, to carry it instead. Subsequently Simon and his family become believers, as his sons Alexander and Rufus are known to Mark and presumably to some of his readers. Rufus may well be the Rufus referred to in Paul's letter to the Romans (see Romans 16:13).

It is nine o'clock when the execution party arrives at the site of execution called Golgotha, a small hill or mound in the shape of a skull. They offer Jesus myrrh, as the wise men or Magi did when he was an infant (Matthew 2:11), to ease the pain, but he refuses to drink it. They divide his clothes between them. And affixed to the cross is a single notice, written, we are told by John, in Aramaic, Latin and Greek (John 19:19–21). It reads "The King of the Jews".

The crucifixion and burial (Mark 15:26–47)

At the twelfth hour (midday), a mood swing comes over the hill at Golgotha. Previously, in their excitement at having Jesus crucified, the chief priests and teachers of the law mocked him, proud of their achievement. Jesus was rendered painfully powerless. They rubbed salt into his wounds with their ironic mockery, "He saved others, but he could not save himself" (Mark 15:31). Their words are precisely true: in the process of saving others, he cannot save himself.

At the twelfth hour, the mood changes. Any feelings of triumph in silencing their enemy have dissipated among the Jewish rulers, faced by the raw horror of crucifixion. Indeed, "many felt tainted by even viewing a crucifixion".[29] Apart from anything else, a fastidious Jew might come too close to death itself to preserve his own ritual purity.

Now it is getting dark: a cloud or eclipse is taking place, and a brooding, eerie darkness envelops the scene. All birdsong is quiet in that desolate place. And Jesus's loud, distinctive cry breaks the stillness, showing that long ago he has discounted the jibes of the Jewish leaders and is involved in a deep struggle of the soul in which he feels himself abandoned, smitten by God and utterly forsaken (Isaiah 53:7–10). Using the opening words of Psalm 22, he cries out: "My God, my God, why have you forsaken me?" The cry reflects the anguish of his soul, rather than the physical torment of his body, which is by now suffering dehydration, exhaustion and growing asphyxiation as he struggles for every breath. The anguish of his soul is that in some mysterious way he has become a guilt offering, despised, rejected, "one from whom people hide their faces" (Isaiah 53:3). But worst of all, one from whom the face of the

Father is entirely hidden. As the Apostle Paul will later say, "God made him who had no sin to be sin for us, so that in him we might become the righteousness of God" (2 Corinthians 5:21). Experiencing this inner travail, he cries out the cry of dereliction. The crowd think he is appealing to Elijah, but Elijah has already come in the person of John the Baptist (Matthew 11:14).

At the same time, even as Jesus breathes his last and cries out, "It is finished" (John 19:30), the curtain in the sanctuary of the Temple is torn from top to bottom (Mark 15:38). This curtain, which was one of two in the Temple, divided the Most Holy Place from the Sanctuary or Holy Place, and normally only once a year, on the Day of Atonement, did the High Priest go through it (see Exodus 26:31–35; Leviticus 16:15, 16). It was there that the Ark of the Covenant with the Law and the mercy seat (a cover) resided, and once a year the High Priest sprinkled the blood of a bull on the mercy seat in an act of atonement. But now, with the curtain torn from top to bottom, and a greater High Priest offering his own blood on the mercy seat of the cross, a new and living way had been found by which humanity might have access to the presence of God (see Hebrews 10:19–25; Romans 3:25; Ephesians 2:18; 3:12). The symbolism of the torn curtain signifies that, through faith in the New Covenant, essentially the person of Jesus and his death, anyone may approach the living God with confidence and freedom.

And finally, in Mark's narrative of the crucifixion, a Roman centurion in charge of the execution party makes a confession: "Truly," he says, "this was the Son of God" (*hyios theou* or *divi filius*). It is the same phrase and ascription given to Jesus at the beginning of the Gospel (1:1). It is the ascription that they are divine falsely given to emperors and inscribed on Roman coins. But here is the true king, acknowledged spontaneously by, of all people, a Roman centurion drawn from an earthly empire. And the witnesses to these universe-changing events are a group of faithful women: Mary Magdalene, Mary the mother of James and Joseph, and Salome. John, the only disciple to remain at the crucifixion, has by now taken Jesus's mother Mary to his home (John 19:25–27).

The final part of Mark's record of that first Good Friday is the burial of Jesus. As the evening approaches and the Sabbath is about to begin (from sunset on Friday evening until sunset on Saturday), a member of

THE CRUCIFIED AND RISEN KING

the Sanhedrin, Joseph of Arimathea, who is already a follower of Jesus, comes out of the closet (so to speak) and boldly approaches Pilate for the body of Jesus. Pilate is surprised that Jesus is already dead and asks the centurion in charge of the execution, and who has already declared Jesus "the Son of God", to confirm that the prisoner is indeed dead. Learning that Jesus has died, quite possibly from a ruptured heart (John 19:33), the body is given into the keeping of Joseph. He wraps it in fresh linen and spices (John 19:39–40) with the help of Nicodemus. They place the body in Joseph's tomb, which is carved out of the rock, and place a stone in front. Mary Magdalene and Mary, the mother of Joseph, watch.

Although it may be considered speculation, it must be true that at the point of death, the divine and eternal spirit of Jesus continued in the godhead of Father, Son and Spirit. In the final moments of his earthly life, we are told he commends his spirit into the hands of the Father (Luke 23:46; John 19:30). Thus, his body dies, but his spirit continues. After all, Peter tells us that "he was put to death in the body but made alive in the Spirit. After being made alive, he went and made proclamation to the imprisoned spirits" (1 Peter 3:18, 19).

So, his lifeless body is lain in the borrowed rich man's tomb, but the eternal Son of God is not extinguished. His body and his spirit wait with all creation for the moment of resurrection.

The resurrection of Jesus

As an end to the Gospel, the words "They said nothing to anyone because they were afraid" (Mark 16:8) clearly present a problem. Before we come to Mark's typically sparse account of the Resurrection, let's address this problem. Was it really Mark's intention to end his Gospel this way? It appears that the shorter ending (e.g., an alternative ninth verse) and the longer ending (vv. 9–16) were added later by a scribe (for instance, an Armenian called Ariston, sometime in the second century).[30] The earliest complete manuscripts, such as *Codex Vaticanus* and *Codex Sinaiticus*, do not have either of these additional endings, whereas later manuscripts do. If they were added later, does that make them genuine Scripture? Probably not, but nothing in these additions is contrary to Scripture, so the scribe did a good job and appears to add to his ending other resurrection stories and Jesus's final command in Matthew to go into all the world and preach the Gospel (Matthew 28:16–20). If we are left with the conclusion that Mark ended his Gospel with "They said nothing to anyone because they were afraid", why was that?

The simple answer is we probably don't know. It might be that Mark suddenly died and did not quite complete the Gospel as he intended. It might be that he was arrested and was separated from his manuscript. It could be that that persecution was the cause of the abrupt ending of the Gospel.[31]

So why end the Gospel in what musicians might call *diminuendo* or *adagio*, rather than *allegro* and *crescendo*? Why a note of fear rather than unalloyed joy and triumph? And why not with the authoritative command of Matthew's Gospel (28:16–20), or the deep anticipation of Luke's Gospel to "stay in the city until you have been clothed with power from on high" (Luke 24:49). By contrast, the women who have been at the tomb, who have seen its emptiness and who have met the angels who told them Christ was alive and going to Galilee (Mark 16:6, 7), were not overcome with joy and confidence but "trembled" and were "bewildered", and this overwhelming experience kept them silent initially: or at least *partially silent*, as we know that Mary Magdalene, the first witness to the resurrection, did go and tell Peter and the disciples (John 20:2, 18). But again, why the muted ending?

Perhaps Mark ends as he does because for very many seeking to grasp the full significance of the Resurrection there is bewilderment and a fog of imperception. Like Peter, Mark's mentor in Rome, Mark is saying that before there is certainty, comprehension and a call to discipleship, there is denial, misunderstanding and fear.[32] The event the women have just witnessed is barely graspable. It is so far beyond their understanding that their joy is muted by incomprehension, their triumph by uncertainty about what this really means.

At first light on Sunday, the first day of the week, the women return to the garden where Jesus has been entombed. They have seen the tomb's location and watched the burial sorrowfully, but thankfully, performed by Joseph and Nicodemus. Now they come at first light to further embalm Jesus, or at least to wrap into his shroud more spices, a gesture of love and devotion. They wonder who will roll away the stone (Mark 16:3). But when they come to the tomb, they find the stone already moved and inside an angel who looks like a young man seated on a ledge on the right side where the body had been. He tells them that Jesus the Nazarene is alive and has gone ahead of them to Galilee (16:7). Not surprisingly, given all that they have witnessed in the last thirty-six hours, they are overwhelmed and scarcely able to take it in.

The empty tomb is the outcome of an event of such universal significance that it is hard to describe. We call it the Resurrection. If you had been inside the tomb and were watching the body before dawn on Sunday morning—what might you have seen? Most likely the sudden disappearance of the body. It is unlikely that Jesus awoke from death, slipped out of his grave clothes and pushed away the stone. No, it was more radical, far-reaching and epoch-making than that. He moved into a new form of existence. Still bearing the scars of his suffering (John 20:27), but in a new and glorious body (1 Corinthians 15:53, 54; Philippians 3:21), he was raised by the Spirit into a new existence, the first fruits of a renewed humanity, no longer subject to death or sin, to establish the kingdom which he inaugurated on earth and now handed to the Father (1 Corinthians 15:20–24). The coming of the kingdom was now irreversible, its progress and triumph assured.

The dawn can come in two ways, either with immediate bright sunlight, dazzling and unmistakeable, or, as sometimes in England, through mist which must clear. It is the same sun, but its rays take time to break through. For the women who had bravely stayed with Jesus through his suffering and crucifixion and who, unlike the apostles, had gone early to the tomb, *the dawn was misty*. There was trembling and bewilderment, fear and silence (Mark 16:8). Often that is the way into certitude, but soon these things would be dispelled by the sun's rays. Mark was confident enough to allow that discovery to be made, but others sought greater emphasis, and a greater *crescendo* to the end of his Gospel.

Group Discussion Questions

Chapter 1: Start as You Mean to Go On

Mark 1

1. If you were writing a Gospel, what would your opening line be? (Perhaps each member could write an opening line and read it out, and say why they have chosen those words.)
2. What do you think of Mark's opening sentence? What do the terms Messiah and Son of God mean to you? What did they mean then?
3. Why did Jesus need an announcer?
4. What is the significance of the baptism of Jesus? What are its three parts? Why was Jesus baptized if he had no sins to repent (1:4)?
5. Did there have to be temptations?
6. What did Jesus mean by saying the kingdom of God has come near?
7. Why was the calling of the disciples so critical to Jesus's mission?
8. How does Jesus demonstrate the proximity of the kingdom in the rest of the chapter?
9. What was so remarkable about Jesus's ministry (see 1:22)?
10. How did Jesus balance activity and reflection or prayer? How do we?

Chapter 2: A New Authority

Mark 2 and 3

1. How did Jesus demonstrate the presence of the kingdom in these two chapters?
2. What might the connection be between the forgiveness of sins and healing? What examples are there of this?
3. Why did the Pharisees object to Jesus saying, "The Son of Man has authority on earth to forgive sins" (2:10)?
4. How are vocations formed today? What made Matthew get up and follow?
5. In relation to fasting and observing the Sabbath, Jesus had remarkable freedom. At what point does a spiritual discipline become a restrictive practice?
6. The formation of a new community lay at the heart of Jesus's strategy. What were to be the principal marks of this new community (see 3:13–34)?

Chapter 3: Growth and Secrecy

Mark 4:1–34

1. In telling these stories about the kingdom of God and its pattern of growth, what was Jesus hoping to achieve?
2. Why did Jesus always speak in parables to the crowds (4:11–12)?
3. Were there any advantages to Jesus in secrecy?
4. What are the main lessons from these growth parables: the Sower, the Growing Seed and the Mustard Seed? How would these lessons help the disciples?
5. The seeds that flourish in the Parable of the Sower are those that develop their root structure and have space to grow. What might that mean for us? What does that look like in practice?

6. How should we communicate the good news of the kingdom today? Is there any place for secrecy, or nuance, or allegory, or is plain speaking best?

Chapter 4: Signs of the Kingdom and the King

Mark 4:35–6:56

The Creation Miracles: Mark 4:35–41; 6:30–56

The Calming of the Storm

1. What are the faith lessons in the miracle of the calming of the storm?
2. What is the relationship between fear and faith? How might that work out in daily living?
3. What effect did this event have on the disciples' understanding of Jesus?

The Feeding of the Five Thousand

1. What was the context of this miracle? How did Jesus resolve the conflict between "rest" for his disciples and "compassion" for the crowd?
2. What did the disciples learn from this event?
3. What other secondary lessons (beside the miraculous feeding of the crowd) may be learnt from this event?

The Walking on the Water

1. If there had been no Lake Galilee, what insights into the attitude and power of Jesus would we have missed?
2. What were the disciples slow to grasp?
3. What aspect of this account particularly strikes you?

The Healing Miracles: Mark 5:1–41; 6:53–56

The Gadarene Demoniac

1. What was the demoniac like before and after this deliverance or healing?
2. What does the obedience of the evil spirits teach us about spiritual conflict?
3. What aspects of the healing of the Gadarene Demoniac do you find difficult?
4. Why do you think the local people wanted Jesus to leave?

The Woman with the Issue of Blood and Jairus's Daughter

1. Why did Jesus make the woman who touched him come into the open?
2. What was Jesus's attitude to death?
3. How was the kingdom of God demonstrated in these healing miracles?

Opportunities and Constraints in Ministry: Mark 6:1–6,7–13,14–29

1. What were the constraints on Jesus in Nazareth, and why should familiarity be restrictive?
2. By contrast, the apostles had a great opportunity; what accounts for the difference in results?
3. What kind of providence is at work in the martyrdom of John the Baptist?
4. As you look back over this section, what is the most striking lesson for you?

Chapter 5: Responses to Jesus

Mark 7:1–8:26

1. In these verses we see the reaction of different people to Jesus: the Pharisees, a Syrophoenician woman, and the disciples. What accounts for such diverse responses?
2. What had the Pharisees at heart got wrong? How was that?
3. How did this fundamental misunderstanding of God's requirement come about (see also Matthew 23:23)?
4. What was Jesus able to make clear to the disciples eventually (see 7:14–23)?
5. What was it, by contrast, that the Syrophoenician woman understood? Is there any accounting for the rightness of her response and the wrongness of the Pharisees' response to Jesus?
6. What did Jesus admire in her?
7. In what ways did the disciples show that they were slow to understand (see 8:4)? And what was Jesus getting at in 8:17–21?
8. There are two healing stories in this section (7:31–35 and 8:22–26). What can we learn from them?
9. What overall lessons might you draw out from this section? What do you think Mark was trying to teach us from these accounts?

Chapter 6: The Turning at the Crossroads

Mark 8:27–9:32

1. Why did Jesus choose to go to Caesarea Philippi?
2. What is the significance of Jesus's question, "Who do you say that I am?"
3. What is our understanding of "Messiah", which is translated by the word Christ in the Greek, meaning Anointed One? What significance did it have in Israel at the time?
4. What is the significance of Peter's declaration that Jesus is the Messiah?

5. Why was Jesus's announcement that he would suffer and die so difficult for Peter to receive? Why was Jesus so severe on him and his response?

6. What do we understand the "way of the cross" to mean? Why is it so often part of Christian discipleship?

7. Can you see why these exchanges should be so quickly followed in the Gospel by the account of the Transfiguration?

8. What is the importance of the Transfiguration to Jesus and to the disciples?

9. What can be learnt from the failure of the disciples to help the boy with the evil spirit?

10. How would you sum up this section of the Gospel?

Chapter 7: The Values of the Kingdom

Mark 9:33–10:45

1. What was going on among the disciples as they walked towards Jerusalem?

2. What can a child teach us?

3. What do we learn from Jesus's saying, "Whoever is not against us is for us"? How do we balance generosity and orthodoxy in our attitudes?

4. Self-discipline, vision, humility, faith and love are key ingredients to discipleship. Why is Jesus so insistent on self-discipline here (9:42ff.)?

5. How can we help marriages to thrive today?

6. What can we learn from the meeting of the Rich Young Ruler and Jesus?

7. Is it necessary to give away everything to be a disciple?

8. Why were the disciples "astonished" (10:32) as they went up to Jerusalem?

9. The disciples were at it again, this time James and John: what did they still have to learn about the kingdom?

10. Is Mark 10:45 the kernel of this Gospel?

Chapter 8: The Wisdom of the King

Mark 10:46–12:44

1. What were the characteristics of Jesus's triumph? How did it differ from a Roman Triumph?
2. What did Jesus have to say about Israel, and how did he say it?
3. How do you understand the judgement of the fig tree?
4. In what ways was the Temple a snare?
5. What are our civic responsibilities and what are our responsibilities towards God?
6. What had the Sadducees got so badly wrong?
7. What was so brilliant about Jesus's answer to the teacher of the law (12:28)?
8. What was the significance of the question that Jesus had for the teachers?
9. Why is the widow so close to Jesus's heart (12:41ff.)?

Chapter 9: The Labour Pains of the Kingdom

Mark 13

1. When you think of the future, what are your main thoughts?
2. The destruction of the Temple did happen in AD 70. What significance does that have for Jesus's teaching on the subject of the future?
3. What are the marks of the epoch leading up to the return of Christ?
4. What are the known knowns and the known unknowns about this period?
5. How are we to live in light of these facts that Jesus gives us?
6. What have Christians often got wrong when thinking about the Second Coming? How can we guard against that?

Chapter 10: The Costly Opening of the Kingdom

Mark 14

1. What do we learn from the anointing of Jesus at Bethany?
2. Why did Jesus earnestly desire to eat the Last Supper with the disciples?
3. What does the Eucharist or Communion service mean for you?
4. Why was Peter so confident in himself (14:27–31)?
5. What did Jesus gain from the agony in the Garden which the disciples lacked?
6. What is the effect of prayer on the flesh (see "the spirit is willing, but the flesh is weak", 14:38)?
7. How did Jesus conduct himself faced by grave injustice at his trial (see 1 Peter 2:23)? What had prepared him for this? What was the irony at the heart of the trial?
8. What happened to Peter in the courtyard? What might he have done to prevent it?

Chapter 11: The Crucified and Risen King

Mark 15 and 16

1. What strikes you about the trial of Jesus before Pilate? What is central to the trial and the scourging of Jesus?
2. What aspects of the crucifixion does Mark especially bring out? What does he want us to understand?
3. What is the significance of the cloud (the darkness), the cry, *Eloi lama sabachthani*, the curtain, and the confession by the centurion?
4. What thoughts do you take from the account of the burial?
5. How do you understand the Resurrection to have occurred? What does it mean for the created order?
6. Why does Mark's Gospel end in the way that it does?
7. Looking back over our studies throughout the Gospel, what principal things will you take away from it?

Notes

1   Stephen J. Davis, *The Early Coptic Papacy: The Egyptian Church and Its Leadership in Late Antiquity* (Cairo: American University of Cairo Press, 2004), p. 6, and Eusebius HE 2.16.1.

2   See Acts 18:2 for the effect of this dismissal of Christians from Rome, which is also recorded by the Roman author, Suetonius.

3   Kallistos Ware, *The Orthodox Way* (New York: St Vladimir's Press, 1995), p. 31.

4   Gregory the Great, *The Book of Pastoral Rule*, tr. George Demacopoulos (New York: St Vladimir's Press, 2007), 2.7, pp. 68–9.

5   Basil of Caesarea, letter 38, Loeb Classical Library, tr. R. J. Deferrari (Cambridge, MA: Harvard University Press, 1926), pp. 197ff.

6   C. S. Lewis, *The Screwtape Letters* (London: Collins, 1983), p. 9.

7   The Apostolic Fathers, *Epistle to Diognetus*, Loeb Classical Library, Vol. 25 (Cambridge, MA: Harvard University Press, 2005), p. 151.

8   St Augustine, *City of God*, tr. Henry Bettenson (London: Penguin, 2003), p. 202.

9   Shoshana Zuboff, *The Age of Surveillance Capitalism* (London: Profile Books, 2019), p. 448.

10   G. K. Chesterton, *Orthodoxy* (London: Hodder and Stoughton, 1999), p. 187. The Serpentine is a lake in Hyde Park.

11   Ibid., p. 240.

12   Mike Mason, *The Mystery of Marriage* (Marc Europe, 1985), p. 71.

13   See "The Marriage Course" at <https://themarriagecourse.org/>, a wonderful tool for enhancing and enriching marriage.

14   Athanasius, *De Incarnatione*, tr. John Behr (New York: SVS Press, 2011), p. 105.

15   Tom Holland, *Dynasty: The Rise and Fall of the House of Caesar* (London: Little, Brown, 2015), p. 66.

16 C. E. B. Cranfield, *The Gospel according to St Mark* (Cambridge: Cambridge University Press, 1966), p. 351.

17 See J. Jeremias, *Jerusalem in the Time of Jesus* (London: SCM Press, 1969), p. 252.

18 Jeremias, *Jerusalem in the Time of Jesus*, p. 337.

19 Cranfield, *St Mark*, p. 377.

20 C. S. Lewis, *Mere Christianity* (London: Fount, 1981), p. 106.

21 Jeremias, *Jerusalem in the Time of Jesus*, pp. 22–3.

22 See Josephus, tr. G. A. Williamson, *The Jewish War* (London: Penguin, 1972), pp. 342ff.

23 Athanasius, *To Serapion On the Holy Spirit*, Epistle 2.9 <http://thegroveisonfire.com/books/Athanasius/Athanasius-Letters-to-Serapion-CRB-Shapland.pdf>.

24 Georgina Battiscombe, *Shaftesbury* (London: Constable, 1974), p. 293.

25 John Calvin, *Institutes of the Christian Religion*, Book IV, Ch. XVII, cap. 3 (Edinburgh: T & T Clark, 1875), p. 558.

26 Fitzroy Maclean, *Eastern Approaches* (London: Penguin, 2009), pp. 80ff.

27 Malcolm Muggeridge, *The Infernal Grove* (London: Fontana, 1973), p. 145.

28 See N. T. Wright, *Paul and the Faithfulness of God*, Part III (London: SPCK, 2013), p. 820.

29 Tom Holland, *Dominion* (London: Little, Brown, 2019), p. xiv.

30 Cranfield, *St Mark*, pp. 471–2.

31 Cranfield, *St Mark*, pp. 8–9.

32 See also Rowan Williams, *Meeting God in Mark* (London: SPCK, 2014), pp. 72ff.

EU GPSR Authorized Representative:

LOGOS EUROPE, 9 rue Nicolas Poussin, 17000 La Rochelle, France

contact@logoseurope.eu

www.ingramcontent.com/pod-product-compliance
Lightning Source LLC
Chambersburg PA
CBHW070332090426
42733CB00012B/2450